THE PITMASTER'S
ELECTRIC SMOKER COOKBOOK

MUST KNOW
PRO TIPS

Mastering Mouthwatering Feasts for Memorable Family Gatherings with Irresistible Recipes

GARRETT SHELTON

TABLE OF CONTENTS

INTRODUCTION

Welcome to "The Pitmaster's Electric Smoker Cookbook," your ultimate guide to mastering the art and science of electric smoking. If you're holding this book, chances are you share my passion for good food, the kind that gathers family and friends around a table, mouths watering, eager for that first succulent bite. Whether you're new to the world of electric smoking or looking to deepen your expertise, I'm here to guide you through every step of the journey.

My own path into the realm of electric smoking began with a simple curiosity and a love for BBQ that runs deep in my family's roots. Like many of you, I started with a basic grill, mastering burgers and steaks, but I always knew that true BBQ magic lay in the slow-cooked, smoke-infused flavors that only patience and practice could perfect. The transition to electric smoking was a game-changer for me. It offered the control and consistency I craved, without sacrificing the authentic smoky taste that defines great BBQ.

Over the years, I've had my share of trial and error, from early successes that brought my family to the table with wide eyes and bigger appetites, to a few smoky misadventures that taught me more than any success ever could. Each experience was a building block, shaping my understanding of electric smoking and fueling my desire to share these discoveries with others.

This book is the culmination of those years of experimentation, learning, and, most importantly, eating. I've poured every tip, trick, and hard-earned lesson into these pages, aiming to demystify the process of electric smoking and make it accessible to everyone. Whether it's choosing the right smoker, selecting wood chips for the perfect flavor profile, or crafting a rub that will make your brisket the star of the next family gathering, I'm here to share what I've learned.

Electric smoking is an art, but it's also a science, one that allows for creativity and personal expression within the bounds of temperature controls and cooking times. It's a journey that invites you to become not just a cook, but a pitmaster, revered by friends and family for your BBQ prowess.

So, whether you're aiming to impress at your next family BBQ, looking to elevate your weekend dinners, or simply exploring the vast and flavorful world of smoked cuisine, consider me your guide. Together, we'll embark on a delicious adventure, transforming ordinary meals into extraordinary memories.

Let's fire up that smoker and get cooking. Welcome to the family.

CHAPTER 1: UNDERSTANDING YOUR ELECTRIC SMOKER

As we embark on this first chapter, we're about to dive deep into the essential groundwork that will set you up for smoking success. From outfitting your electric smoker with the must-have accessories to understanding the key safety and maintenance protocols, this chapter lays the foundation. Equipped with this knowledge, you'll be well-prepared to master the art of smoking, creating dishes that tantalize the taste buds and gather everyone around the table for a memorable feast.

ESSENTIAL ELECTRIC SMOKER ACCESSORIES

Once you've bought your electric smoker, it's like you've just adopted a new member of the family. And just like any family member, you want to make sure it has everything it needs to thrive. That's where accessories come into play. Think of them as the secret sauce to your smoking success. Let's dive into the essential electric smoker accessories that will take your smoking game from "pretty good" to "can't-stop-eating-this" levels of delicious.

THE MUST-HAVE MEAT THERMOMETER

First on the list, and non-negotiable in my book, is a good meat thermometer. The kind that makes guessing if your meat is done a thing of the past. I've had my fair share of "is it cooked?" moments, and believe me, a reliable meat thermometer is a lifesaver. Whether you prefer a simple probe or a fancy digital model with Bluetooth, ensuring you're cooking your meat to the perfect temperature is crucial for both safety and taste.

The ThermoPro TP20 Wireless Remote Digital Cooking Food Meat Thermometer is celebrated for its accuracy and ease of use, offering peace of mind whether you're smoking brisket or chicken. Its wireless capability means you can monitor your smoke from a distance, ensuring precision without being tethered to your smoker.

QUALITY WOOD CHIPS

Next up, wood chips. They're the essence of smoking, the very heart and soul. Investing in quality wood chips will make all the difference in the flavor of your smoked delicacies. Experiment with different types—hickory for a classic BBQ taste, applewood for a sweeter touch, or mesquite for a bold kick. Remember, it's like choosing the right seasoning for your steak; the right wood chips can elevate your dish to new heights.

Brands like Weber and Traeger offer a variety of premium wood chips and pellets, from hickory and mesquite to apple and cherry.

A TRUSTY SMOKER COVER

Now, let's talk about protection—smoker cover protection, that is. Your electric smoker is going to be one of your best friends, so you'll want to keep it safe from the elements. A good smoker cover will shield your precious smoker from rain, snow, and even the occasional bird dropping. It's the knight in shining armor for your smoker, keeping it clean and ready for your next smoking session.

RIB RACKS AND FISH BASKETS

For those who love ribs and fish, rib racks and fish baskets are your new best friends. Rib racks maximize space, allowing you to smoke more ribs at once, which is a game-changer for big gatherings. Fish baskets, on the other hand, keep your delicate fish from flaking apart and provide an easy way to flip them without any casualties. The first time I used a fish basket, it was a revelation—no more pieces of salmon sticking to the grates!

A RELIABLE SMOKER BOX (FOR PELLET SMOKERS)

And if you're diving into the world of pellet smokers, a quality smoker box is key. It helps keep your pellets dry and ready to smoke, ensuring consistent smoke production and flavor. There's nothing quite like the panic of finding your pellets have turned into a soggy mess right when you're ready to start smoking.

The Smokehouse Products Smoker Box is a versatile option that can be used with any grill or smoker, including electric models, to add that extra layer of smoky goodness to your dishes.

SILICONE GLOVES: THE UNSUNG HEROES

Lastly, let's not forget about silicone gloves. These unsung heroes protect your hands from the heat, making handling hot trays and food a breeze. Furthermore, they're much easier to clean than traditional fabric gloves. After a close encounter with a hot tray and a pair of fabric gloves, I switched to silicone, and my hands (and laundry) have thanked me ever since.

Armed with these essential accessories, you're not just ready to smoke; you're ready to impress. Each one adds a layer of convenience, safety, and flavor to your smoking experience. So gear up, because your electric smoking adventures are about to get a whole lot tastier.

SAFETY TIPS AND MAINTENANCE FOR LONGEVITY

The journey of electric smoking is filled with the aroma of smoked meats and the satisfaction of mastering a new culinary skill. But, like any great adventure, it's important to travel safely and keep your trusty gear in tip-top shape. Let's chat about keeping you, your electric smoker, and your delicious smoked treats all happily humming along.

SAFETY FIRST: A NON-SMOKING AREA

First and foremost, safety isn't just a catchy phrase; it's a must. I learned this the hard way when I was just starting out and nearly turned my smoker into a makeshift campfire. Remember, even though it's an electric smoker, it's still generating a lot of heat. Make sure it's placed on a stable, non-flammable surface and away from any structures or materials that could catch fire. And, of course, keep it out of reach of children and pets. We want to smoke the brisket, not the tail of Mr. Whiskers.

THE CLEAN MACHINE: MAINTENANCE 101

Keeping your smoker clean isn't just about hygiene; it's about performance. A clean smoker is a happy smoker, and a happy smoker means better tasting food. After each use, give it a good wipe down to remove any grease or food particles. Pay special attention to the racks and the inside of the smoker box. Occasionally, you'll want to do a deeper clean, getting into all the nooks and crannies. Trust me, the effort you put into maintaining your smoker will pay off in the longevity of your device and the quality of your smoked meals.

THE GREAT OUTDOORS: WEATHERPROOFING

Electric smokers love the great outdoors, but they're not exactly fans of water. If you're smoking in an area that might get a bit of rain, or if you're storing your smoker outside, make sure it's properly covered. Water and electronics are a mix about as good as oil and water. I once had a smoker that got a little too much love from a surprise rainstorm, and it was like trying to start a car underwater. Learn from my mishap: keep your smoker dry and covered when not in use.

THE SEASONED SMOKER: A LITTLE LOVE GOES A LONG WAY

Lastly, don't forget to season your smoker. No, I'm not talking about salt and pepper; I'm talking about coating the inside with cooking oil and running it at a high temperature for a couple of hours. This helps protect the interior, preventing rust and creating a non-stick surface. It's like seasoning a cast-iron skillet—the more you do it, the better it performs.

Remember, taking care of your electric smoker isn't just about maintenance; it's about ensuring every smoking session is as good as the first. Plus, it's a great way to show a little love to your faithful cooking companion.

As we transition from understanding the foundational elements of your electric smoker and the essential accessories that elevate your smoking game, let's turn up the heat on our culinary journey. Mastering the basics sets the stage for the artistry of smoking, where time, temperature, and the choice of smoke flavor blend harmoniously to create dishes that are not just meals, but experiences. With the tools and knowledge in hand, you're now ready to delve into the nuances of mastering the smoke, where the true magic of transforming simple ingredients into unforgettable delights awaits in Chapter 2.

CHAPTER 2: THE BASICS OF ELECTRIC SMOKING

Diving into the world of electric smoking can feel a bit like stepping into a spacecraft for the first time—there are buttons, dials, and compartments that all play a crucial role in the journey to flavor town. But don't worry; you won't need a pilot's license to operate your electric smoker. Let's break down how these marvelous machines work, making the complex beautifully simple.

THE HEART OF THE OPERATION: HEATING ELEMENTS

At the core of every electric smoker is the heating element—think of it as the heart, pumping out heat instead of blood. This element is what sets the electric smoker apart from its fire-fueled cousins. With the twist of a dial or the press of a button, you're in control, dictating the temperature with precision that would make a Swiss watchmaker nod in approval. I remember my first time setting the temperature on my smoker; I felt like a DJ, mixing the beats of heat to get the perfect smoke.

THE LUNGS: WOOD CHIPS AND SMOKE

Now, where does that irresistible smoky flavor come from? Enter the wood chips, the lungs of the operation. These are placed in a tray or container near the heating element. As the element heats up, so do the chips, beginning to smolder and release smoke—this is the magic, the alchemy of smoking. Unlike traditional smoking methods that require constant monitoring of wood and flames, your electric smoker takes care of the smoke level, letting you focus on the anticipation of the feast to come.

THE CIRCULATORY SYSTEM: VENTS AND AIRFLOW

Just like lungs need oxygen, your smoker needs airflow to keep the smoke moving. This is where vents come into play, acting as the circulatory system of your smoker. They help regulate the smoke density and temperature inside the chamber. Adjusting the vents can feel a bit like finding the perfect balance in a seesaw—with a little practice, you'll know just where to set them to achieve the smoky flavor you're after without turning your meat into a charcoal briquette.

THE SKELETON: RACKS AND TRAYS

Holding everything together inside your electric smoker are the racks and trays, the skeleton of your machine. These allow you to organize your meats and vegetables like a seasoned librarian, ensuring everything has its place for optimal smoke exposure. The beauty of these racks is their versatility—whether you're smoking a batch of jalapeño poppers or a whole turkey, there's a configuration that fits. And yes, there's a certain joy in sliding those racks out, revealing the smoked treasures that await.

THE BRAIN: DIGITAL CONTROLS AND TIMERS

For those who love gadgets and gizmos, the digital controls and timers on many electric smokers are like having a mini-computer dedicated to your culinary success. These features take the guesswork out of smoking, allowing you to set the temperature and timer and then, in the wise words of many a pitmaster, "leave it and love it." I've spent many smoke sessions marveling at how technology has transformed the art of smoking into a science of flavor.

Understanding how your electric smoker works is the first step in mastering it. With this knowledge, you're not just operating a machine; you're orchestrating a symphony of heat, smoke, and timing to create something truly delicious. So, as you embark on this smoky journey, remember: behind every great smoked dish is a curious cook, a handful of wood chips, and the marvel of modern smoking technology.

THE ART OF TEMPERATURE CONTROL

Temperature control is the secret sauce of the smoking world! If smoking were a dance, temperature control would be the rhythm that keeps everything moving smoothly. It's what separates the newbies from the seasoned pitmasters. But fear not, my friend, for mastering this art is more about understanding your partner (the electric smoker) than performing complex footwork.

THE DANCE BEGINS

Think of your electric smoker as a dance floor where the temperature sets the beat. Too hot, and you're at a salsa club in the middle of summer—everything's overcooked and sweaty. Too cool, and you're slow-dancing in a freezer, where nothing ever gets done. The goal is to find that sweet spot, where the heat is just right, and the smoke gently waltzes around your food.

LEARNING THE STEPS: TEMPERATURE RANGES

Every type of food has its preferred dancing style, or in smoking terms, its ideal temperature range. For instance, brisket and pork shoulders love a slow dance, thriving at temperatures between 225°F and 250°F. Fish, on the other hand, prefers a quicker step, best smoked around 175°F to 200°F. It's all about matching the temperature to the food's pace. I remember my first brisket; I treated it like a sprint rather than a marathon. Let's just say, it was more of a learning experience than a culinary success. But don't worry. In the next chapters you will get a complete temperature and time chart for the most popular foods. This way you can learn the lesson without the scar.

THE LEAD: YOUR ELECTRIC SMOKER'S THERMOSTAT

In this dance, your electric smoker's thermostat leads, guiding the temperature with precision. Unlike traditional smokers, where you're constantly adjusting vents and adding fuel, electric smokers let you set your desired temperature with the turn of a knob or the press of a button. It's like having a dance instructor there to correct your steps, ensuring you're always on beat.

THE RHYTHM: MONITORING AND ADJUSTING

Even with the best electric smokers, it's crucial to keep an ear on the music, so to speak. External factors like outdoor temperature, wind, and even the amount of food inside can affect the smoker's internal temperature. Keep a digital thermometer handy to double-check the smoker's reading, ensuring your food is smoking at the correct pace. There's a certain peace of mind that comes from knowing exactly what's happening inside your smoker, like having a secret window into the world of flavor development.

Mastering the art of temperature control in electric smoking isn't about following strict rules; it's about understanding the rhythm of heat and smoke, and how they interact with your food. With a bit of practice and patience, you'll be leading the dance in no time, producing smoked masterpieces that have everyone asking for an encore.

WOOD CHIPS, CHUNKS, AND PELLETS: CHOOSING THE RIGHT SMOKE FLAVOR

Ah, the world of wood chips, chunks, and pellets—where the magic of smoke transforms simple ingredients into culinary masterpieces. Navigating this world can be akin to choosing the perfect spice for your dish; the right choice can elevate your meal to legendary status.

THE AROMA ORCHESTRA: WOOD CHIPS

Let's start with wood chips, the most commonly used smoke conductor in electric smokers. These little morsels of wood are like the violins in an orchestra—subtle, yet powerful, capable of setting the mood without overwhelming the senses. From the sweet melodies of applewood to the deep bass notes of mesquite, each type of wood chip brings its unique flavor profile to the table.

I remember my first dance with applewood chips; I was smoking a batch of chicken wings. The result was a symphony of sweet, mellow smoke that had everyone asking for an encore. The lesson? Never underestimate the power of choosing the right wood chips. They can make or break your smoking session.

THE BOLD SOLOISTS: WOOD CHUNKS

For those longer smoking sessions, wood chunks step onto the stage. Think of them as the solo artists in the aroma orchestra—bolder and more pronounced, capable of sustaining their flavor over many hours. Using chunks is like adding a dash of audacity to your dish, perfect for larger cuts of meat that need time to develop deep, complex flavors.

One of my fondest memories involves a hefty brisket and a generous helping of hickory chunks. The smoke infused the meat with such a rich, savory flavor that it became the stuff of legend in my family. That brisket didn't just feed us; it told a story of patience, boldness, and the art of smoke.

THE VERSATILE ACCOMPANISTS: PELLETS

And then, we have pellets—a relatively new addition to the smoking world but no less important. Pellets offer a versatility unmatched by chips or chunks, allowing for a broader range of flavors and a more controlled smoking experience. They're like the percussion section of the orchestra, providing a steady, consistent background that supports and enhances the overall performance.

My first venture with pellets involved a salmon filet and a blend of alder and cherry. The combination created a delicate balance of sweetness and smokiness that elevated the salmon from simple to sublime.

CHOOSING YOUR FLAVOR SYMPHONY

Choosing the right smoke flavor is about understanding the character of your dish and the story you want it to tell. Here is a useful table that can help you decide which wood is right for what you are about to cook.

Wood Type	Flavor Profile	Perfect For
Apple	Mild and sweet	Chicken, pork, and fish
Cherry	Slightly sweet and fruity	Poultry, pork, and beef
Hickory	Strong and hearty	Beef, pork, and poultry
Mesquite	Very strong and earthy	Beef and game meats
Oak	Medium to strong, versatile	Beef, pork, and fish
Alder	Mild, with a hint of sweetness	Fish and poultry

Maple	Mild and slightly sweet	Poultry and vegetables
Pecan	Rich and nutty	Pork and poultry
Walnut	Strong and slightly bitter	Red meats and game
Beech	Mild and versatile	Poultry, fish, and seafood
Cedar	Strong, aromatic	Fish, chicken
Plum	Mildly sweet, fruity	Poultry, pork
Applewood	Mild, slightly sweet	Chicken, pork, and fish

Remember, every piece of wood tells a story, and each smoke session is an opportunity to write your own culinary tale. So, whether you're a fan of the subtle notes of wood chips, the bold flavors of chunks, or the versatility of pellets, embrace the journey. After all, the heart of electric smoking lies in the joy of discovery, one smoky note at a time.

As we've navigated through the essentials of electric smoking, mastering the technicalities and understanding the importance of preparation, we're perfectly poised to take our smoking journey to the next level. With our foundation firmly set, let's venture into the realm of fine-tuning our smoking techniques, ensuring every dish not only tastes divine but also presents with perfection. Join me in Chapter 3, where we'll dive deeper into the art of preparing to smoke, transforming good food into great smoked masterpieces with the right selection and preparation of meats and other foods.

CHAPTER 3: PREPARING TO SMOKE

SELECTING THE BEST MEATS FOR SMOKING

This is where our smoky adventure truly begins. It's like casting for a blockbuster movie; choosing the right star can make all the difference. Whether you're a seasoned pitmaster or just starting to explore the smoky world, knowing which meats to spotlight in your electric smoker can turn a simple meal into a show-stopping feast.

THE BRISKET: THE MARATHON RUNNER

Let's kick things off with brisket, the marathon runner of the smoking world. This cut is all about endurance, taking its sweet time to reach that perfect tenderness. Brisket has taught me patience and the art of slow reward. It's a bit of a tough character at first, but with the right preparation and time in the smoker, it transforms into something incredibly tender and flavorful. When choosing a brisket, look for good marbling—the fat is where all the flavor hides. Remember, a little fat can lead to a lot of flavor.

PORK SHOULDER: THE CROWD PLEASER

Next up is pork shoulder, also known as the Boston butt. This cut is the life of the party, always ready to please a crowd with its succulent, fall-apart texture. My first encounter with smoking a pork shoulder was for a family reunion, and let's just say, it made me the hero of the day. The key to a good pork shoulder is selecting one with a nice fat cap and plenty of meat. It's forgiving, making it perfect for beginners, and versatile enough for a variety of dishes, from pulled pork sandwiches to tacos.

RIBS: THE FLAVOR CONDUCTOR

Ah, ribs, the conductor of flavor in the smoking symphony. Whether you prefer baby back or St. Louis style, ribs are all about the harmony between meat, smoke, and seasoning. I still remember the first time I smoked ribs, meticulously rubbing them with my secret blend of spices. The result? A flavor so rich and deep, it was like discovering a new color. When selecting ribs, look for even thickness and a good meat-to-bone ratio. And don't forget the membrane on the back; removing it ensures the smoke and rub penetrate every nook and cranny.

CHICKEN: THE VERSATILE VIRTUOSO

Chicken might seem like a simple choice, but in the world of smoking, it's a versatile virtuoso. From whole chickens to thighs and wings, each cut offers a unique canvas for smoke and seasoning. My adventure with smoked chicken began with a whole bird, brined and then smoked to perfection. The skin was crispy, the meat juicy and infused with a gentle smokiness that was utterly irresistible. For chicken, look for pieces that are uniform in size for even cooking and consider brining for extra juiciness.

THE SUPPORTING CAST: BEEF RIBS, LAMB, AND MORE

Beyond these stars, there's a whole supporting cast waiting to shine in your smoker. Beef ribs with their meaty richness, lamb shoulders offering a tender, flavorful alternative, and even sausages for a quick smokey treat. Each has its unique qualities, but the common thread is quality. Always opt for the best you can afford, as the quality of the meat greatly influences the final outcome.

Selecting the best meats for smoking is about understanding the characteristics of each cut and how they interact with smoke and time. So, take your time, choose wisely, and remember—every great meal starts with great ingredients.

PREPARATION TECHNIQUES: BRINING, MARINATING, AND RUBS

This is where the real magic happens in the kitchen before the smoker even gets warmed up. Think of brining, marinating, and rubbing as the pre-game show, setting the stage for the flavors that will soon dance across your taste buds. Let's dive into these essential techniques that can elevate your smoking game from good to unforgettable.

BRINING: THE MOISTURE MAGICIAN

Brining is like giving your meats a spa day before the big event, ensuring they come out of the smoker juicier and more flavorful than you ever imagined possible. It's all about osmosis, submerging your meat in a solution of water, salt, and often sugar, plus any other spices your heart desires. The salt works its magic, helping the meat retain moisture during the long smoking process.

I'll never forget my first brined chicken. I was skeptical at first—how could a simple saltwater bath make that much of a difference? Oh, how wrong I was. The chicken emerged from the smoker so succulent and flavorful, it was like discovering a new dimension of taste. For a basic brine, mix 1 cup of salt with 1 gallon of water, add your favorite seasonings, and let the meat soak for a few hours or overnight. The result? Unbelievably tender and juicy meat that'll have your guests begging for your secrets.

Step-by-Step Guide to Brining
- **Prepare the Brine Solution**: Start by dissolving 1 cup of salt in 1 gallon of warm water in a large container. If you're using sugar, add it at this stage as well. For every gallon of water, adding up to a cup of sugar can balance the saltiness and add a subtle sweetness to the meat.
- **Add Flavors**: Add your favorite seasonings to the brine solution. Consider garlic cloves, peppercorns, bay leaves, citrus slices, fresh herbs, or even a splash of apple cider vinegar to introduce complex flavors. Stir well to ensure all the elements are well combined.
- **Submerge the Meat**: Place your meat in the brine solution, ensuring it is completely submerged. For larger cuts, you may need to use a weight or a plate to keep the meat under the surface. Make sure to use a non-reactive container (such as plastic, glass, or stainless steel) to avoid any unwanted chemical reactions with the brine.
- **Refrigerate**: Cover the container with a lid or plastic wrap and refrigerate. The brining time varies depending on the type and size of the meat. Generally, a few hours for smaller cuts like chicken breasts or fish, overnight for whole chickens or large pork cuts, and up to 24 hours for whole turkeys.
- **Rinse and Dry**: After brining, remove the meat from the solution and rinse it under cold water to remove excess salt from the surface. Pat the meat dry with paper towels. This step is crucial for achieving that perfect skin texture in the smoker, as a dry surface will better absorb smoke and develop a more appealing crust.
- **Rest Before Smoking**: Let the meat sit after drying for a bit to allow it to come to a more even temperature, which promotes more uniform cooking.

MARINATING: THE FLAVOR INFUSER

Marinating is like sending your meats on a flavor vacation, soaking them in a mixture of oil, acid (like vinegar or citrus juice), and spices. This not only tenderizes the meat but infuses it with deep, complex flavors. The key to a great marinade is balance—finding the right harmony between acidity, oil, and seasonings to complement the natural taste of the meat.

One of my favorite marinades is a simple mix of olive oil, lemon juice, garlic, rosemary, and a touch of honey—perfect for a smoked leg of lamb. The trick is to let the meat marinate long enough to soak up all those delicious flavors, usually at least a few hours or, even better, overnight. Just remember, the longer the marination, the more flavorful the celebration.

Step-by-Step Guide to Marinating
- **Choose Your Base**: Start with a good quality oil as the base of your marinade. Olive oil is a popular choice due to its flavor and health benefits, but you can also use canola, avocado, or any other oil that suits your taste preference. The oil helps to keep the meat moist during cooking and allows the flavors of the spices and seasonings to adhere to the meat.

- **Add Acidity**: Next, incorporate an acid to help tenderize the meat. Lemon juice, lime juice, vinegar, yogurt, or wine are excellent options. The acid breaks down the proteins in the meat, allowing the flavors to penetrate deeply. A good rule of thumb is a 3:1 ratio of oil to acid.
- **Incorporate Aromatics and Seasonings**: This is where you can get creative. Add minced garlic, chopped herbs like rosemary, thyme, or cilantro, and spices such as paprika, cumin, or black pepper. Sweet elements like honey or brown sugar can balance the acidity and add depth. Don't forget to add salt, but be mindful of the amount, especially if you plan to marinate for a long time.
- **Mix Your Marinade**: Combine all your ingredients in a bowl and whisk them together until well blended. Taste the marinade and adjust the seasoning according to your preference. Remember, the marinade should be slightly bolder in taste than what you want your meat to taste like, as not all of it will penetrate the meat.
- **Prepare Your Meat**: For the best results, start with dry meat. Pat your meat dry with paper towels to remove any excess moisture.
- **Marinate**: Place your meat in a ziplock bag or a non-reactive container (glass, plastic, or stainless steel) and pour the marinade over it. Make sure the meat is fully submerged and covered from all sides. Seal the bag or cover the container.
- **Refrigerate**: Marinate in the refrigerator, not at room temperature, to prevent bacterial growth. Small cuts like chicken breasts or fish fillets need only a few hours, while larger pieces like a whole chicken or a leg of lamb can benefit from marinating overnight or up to 24 hours.
- **Turn Occasionally**: If possible, turn the meat halfway through the marinating time to ensure even flavor absorption.

RUBS: THE CRUST CREATORS

And then we have rubs, the superheroes of the smoking world, ready to battle blandness with their potent mix of spices and herbs. Whether you're team dry rub or wet rub, the goal is the same: to create a flavorful crust that will seal in the juices and pack every bite with taste. Dry rubs are a blend of spices and herbs rubbed directly onto the meat, while wet rubs add a bit of oil or sauce to the mix, clinging to the meat with a paste-like consistency.

My first experiment with rubs was a bold mixture of paprika, brown sugar, garlic powder, and a hint of cayenne pepper, rubbed onto a rack of ribs. As the ribs smoked, the rub transformed into a glorious crust that was the perfect balance of sweet, spicy, and smoky. The lesson learned? Don't be afraid to get creative with your rubs—the bolder, the better.

Step-by-Step Guide to Creating and Applying Dry Rubs
- **Select Your Spices and Herbs**: Begin with a base of salt and pepper, then add layers of flavor with paprika, garlic powder, onion powder, dried herbs (such as thyme, rosemary, or oregano), and a touch of heat with cayenne or chili powder. For sweetness, consider brown sugar or dried fruit powders.
- **Mix Your Ingredients**: In a bowl, combine all your spices and herbs. For a basic rub, start with equal parts of each spice and adjust according to taste. If using sugar, be mindful of its burning point and how it will be cooked to avoid a bitter char.
- **Application**: Pat your meat dry with paper towels to ensure the rub sticks well. Generously coat all sides of the meat with the rub, using your hands to press and adhere the spices into every nook. Let the meat sit for at least 15 minutes before cooking, allowing the flavors to meld.

Step-by-Step Guide to Creating and Applying Wet Rubs
- **Prepare Your Base**: Start with the same spices as a dry rub, but add a wet ingredient to bind them together. This can be olive oil, mustard, soy sauce, Worcestershire sauce, or even yogurt for a tenderizing effect.
- **Combine Ingredients**: In a bowl, mix your spices with your chosen wet ingredient until it forms a paste. Adjust the consistency with more liquid or spices as needed. The paste should be thick enough to cling to the meat but not so thick that it's difficult to spread.
- **Application**: As with a dry rub, start by drying the meat with paper towels. Apply the wet rub generously over the meat, massaging it in to ensure good coverage. Allow the meat to sit for at least 30 minutes before cooking, if not marinating it beforehand.

CHAPTER 4: MASTERING THE SMOKE

SMOKING TIMES AND TEMPERATURE CHARTS

Welcome to the heart of the smoky kingdom, where time and temperature reign supreme! Mastering these two elements is like holding the keys to the smokehouse; it unlocks the door to consistently delicious, perfectly smoked dishes. Let's dive into the world of smoking times and temperature charts, your trusty guides on this flavorful journey.

Imagine time and temperature as dance partners in the tango of smoking. It's all about finding that perfect balance, where each step and turn is precisely timed and executed. Too fast or too hot, and your meal might end up more like a rushed cha-cha than a graceful tango. That's where our charts come in, acting as the choreographer for your smoking session, ensuring every move is perfectly planned.

MEAT SMOKING CHART

Food	Temperature	Time Per Pound	Total Time	Internal Temp
Brisket	225°F	1 to 1.5 hours	Varies	N/A
Pork Shoulder	225°F	1 to 1.5 hours	Varies	195°F
Ribs (Baby Back)	225°F	N/A	4 to 5 hours	N/A
Ribs (St. Louis Style)	225°F	N/A	5 to 6 hours	N/A
Chicken (Whole)	250°F	N/A	About 4 hours	165°F
Turkey (Whole)	240°F	N/A	6 to 8 hours	165°F
Beef Ribs	225°F	N/A	6 to 8 hours	203°F
Pork Loin	225°F	1.5 to 2 hours	Varies	145°F

Lamb Shoulder	225°F	1 to 1.5 hours	Varies	195°F
Duck	225°F	N/A	3 to 4 hours	165°F
Venison	225°F	1 to 1.5 hours	Varies	160°F
Sausages	225°F	N/A	1 to 2 hours	160°F
Meatloaf	250°F	N/A	3 to 4 hours	160°F
Ham (Uncooked)	225°F	N/A	5 to 7 hours	160°F
Cornish Hens	250°F	N/A	About 2 hours	165°F
Salmon (Filet)	225°F	N/A	1 to 2 hours	145°F
Trout	225°F	N/A	1 to 2 hours	145°F
Beef Chuck Roast	225°F	1 to 1.5 hours	Varies	190°F
Pork Belly	225°F	N/A	2.5 to 3 hours	200°F
Quail	225°F	N/A	1.5 to 2 hours	165°F

VEGETABLE AND OTHER FOODS SMOKING CHART

Food	Temperature	Time	Notes
Vegetables (General)	225°F to 250°F	1 to 2 hours	Depends on the vegetable and desired smokiness
Cheese (General)	Below 90°F (Cold Smoke)	2 to 4 hours	Cheese doesn't need heat, just smoke flavor
Nuts (Almonds, Pecans)	225°F	1 to 2 hours	Stir occasionally for even smoke
Hard-Boiled Eggs	225°F	2 to 3 hours	For a smoky twist on deviled eggs
Garlic	225°F	2 to 3 hours	For smoked garlic butter
Tomatoes	225°F	2 to 3 hours	For smoky sauces and salsas
Peaches	225°F	1.5 to 2.5 hours	For desserts or savory pairings
Pineapple	225°F	2 to 3 hours	For a smoky sweet treat
Olives	225°F	1 to 2 hours	For a unique addition to salads and martinis
Mushrooms	225°F	1 to 2 hours	For a smoky, meaty texture

Salt	Below 90°F (Cold Smoke)	2 to 4 hours	For a smoky seasoning
Tofu	225°F	1.5 to 2.5 hours	For a smoky vegan protein
Bell Peppers	225°F	1 to 2 hours	For smoky stuffed peppers
Onions	225°F	2 to 3 hours	For adding to dishes or making smoked onion jam
Potatoes	225°F	2 to 3 hours	For a smoky twist on baked potatoes
Asparagus	225°F	1 to 1.5 hours	For a smoky side dish
Carrots	225°F	1.5 to 2.5 hours	For adding a smoky sweetness to dishes
Beets	225°F	2 to 3 hours	For salads or as a side
Apples	225°F	1.5 to 2.5 hours	For desserts or smoked apple sauce

Creating a personalized smoking times and temperature chart is like drafting your dance card for the evening. Start with the basics provided here, then adjust based on your smoker, the outside temperature, and your flavor preferences. I've got a chart that's covered in notes, adjustments, and a few smudges of barbecue sauce—a testament to many smoking adventures.

Remember, these charts are guides, not strict rules. I once tried to smoke a brisket on a whim, without checking my chart, and let's just say it turned into a 24-hour dance-a-thon. But, it was one of the best briskets I've ever had. It taught me that patience and a willingness to go with the flow can lead to unexpectedly delightful results.

So, arm yourself with these charts, a good thermometer, and a sense of adventure.

THE SECRET TO PERFECT SMOKE RINGS

Ah, the elusive smoke ring – that thin band of pinkish-red hue just beneath the surface of your smoked meats, a badge of honor among pitmasters and a visual feast for anyone who beholds it. The smoke ring is the smoke signal of the BBQ world, signaling that yes, indeed, you've mastered the art of smoking. But fear not, dear reader, for this secret is not kept in a vault, accessible only to the BBQ elite. Today, I'm here to share with you the keys to unlocking that coveted symbol of smoky perfection.

First, let's talk science, but don't worry – I'll keep it light. The smoke ring forms when nitrogen dioxide from wood smoke meets the myoglobin in meat, preserving that lovely pink color. It's like a little chemistry love affair right there in your smoker. The reaction happens at the outer edges of the meat, creating that distinctive ring we all crave. Now, while electric smokers excel in many areas, creating a smoke ring can be a bit more challenging due to the clean combustion process. But, where there's a will (and a bit of ingenuity), there's a way.

THE WOOD CHIP WALTZ

Starting with wood chips, the dance partners of your electric smoker, choosing the right type can sway your chances of achieving a smoke ring. Hardwoods like hickory, oak, and mesquite are rich in nitrogen compounds, making them ideal candidates for your smoke ring endeavors. It's like choosing the right shoes for dancing; the better the fit, the smoother the glide.

KEEPING IT COOL

Temperature plays a pivotal role in the formation of a smoke ring. The chemical reaction that creates the smoke ring stops once the meat reaches about 140°F. So, the trick is to keep things cool at the start of your smoke session. Consider placing a tray of ice in the smoker, or chilling your meat before it hits the grate. This slows down the cooking process, giving you a larger window for the smoke ring to develop. It's a bit like slow-dancing in the moonlight, where taking your time makes the moment all the more magical.

MOISTURE: THE CATALYST

Moisture on the surface of the meat can also enhance smoke ring formation. It allows more smoke to adhere to the meat, increasing the potential for that chemical reaction. A simple spritz of water, apple juice, or even a thin layer of mustard before applying your rub can do the trick. It's like setting the stage for our chemistry love affair, making sure everything is just right for the magic to happen.

THE CHARCOAL CHEAT

Now, for those purists who might gasp at the thought, hear me out. Adding a small piece of lit charcoal to your wood chip tray can introduce those nitrogen compounds necessary for a smoke ring. This little "cheat" bridges the gap between traditional and electric smoking, bringing the best of both worlds to your electric smoker. It's a bit like sneaking a professional dancer into your routine to spice things up.

At the end of the day, while the smoke ring is a coveted trophy in the smoking world, it's the taste that truly matters. I've had smoke rings as wide as rivers and times when the ring was as elusive as a shadow in the night. Yet, each time, the flavor spoke louder than any visual cue ever could. So, while you chase the perfect smoke ring, remember to savor the flavors and aromas that make smoking such a rewarding endeavor.

There you have it, the not-so-secret anymore to achieving that perfect smoke ring in your electric smoker. With a little science, some cool tricks, and a lot of patience, you're well on your way to smoking meats that not only taste incredible but look the part too.

HOW TO ACHIEVE CRISPY SKIN AND TENDER MEAT

The eternal quest for the holy grail of smoking: achieving that perfectly crispy skin encasing tender, juicy meat. It's like trying to find the perfect balance between a crunchy exterior and a soul-warming, flavorful interior. But fret not, my fellow smoke enthusiasts, for this quest is not as daunting as it might seem. Let's embark on this journey together, armed with tips and tricks that will lead us to the promised land of crispy skin and tender meat.

THE SECRET OF THE SKIN

First off, let's talk poultry, where the quest for crispy skin is most fervent. The key to achieving that desirable crunch lies in moisture control. Yes, while we often talk about keeping things moist and juicy, when it comes to skin, we want to do the opposite. Here's a little trick I learned: after brining or marinating your bird, let it sit uncovered in the refrigerator for a few hours or even overnight. This dries out the skin, setting the stage for that crisp finish. It's like letting the skin prepare itself for its moment in the spotlight.

THE LOW AND SLOW APPROACH

For tender meat, the mantra is "low and slow." Cooking at a lower temperature for a longer period allows the connective tissues in tougher cuts of meat to break down, transforming them into melt-in-your-mouth morsels of joy. But here's where it gets interesting – to achieve crispy skin on our poultry, we need to introduce a bit of a plot twist towards the end of our smoking session.

After smoking your meat at a lower temperature to achieve tenderness, crank up the heat for the final act. Increasing the temperature of your electric smoker or finishing the meat on a grill or in a hot oven for a short period can crisp up the skin without overcooking the interior. It's a delicate dance, a brief tango with the flames, that elevates the dish from great to unforgettable.

THE ROLE OF RUBS

When it comes to achieving that perfect exterior, don't underestimate the power of a good rub. A mixture containing a bit of sugar can caramelize on the surface, contributing to the crispiness of the skin. Just be mindful of the temperature, as sugar can burn if it's too hot. Think of it as seasoning your way to success, with each granule of salt or sugar playing its part in the symphony of flavors.

Having journeyed through the realms of mastering the smoke, uncovering the secrets behind perfect smoke rings, and achieving the delicate balance of crispy skin with tender meat, we now stand at the precipice of culinary delight. As we turn the page, prepare your taste buds for an adventure, as the next chapter unveils a treasure trove of tasty recipes that will bring all your newfound knowledge to life in the most delicious way possible.

HICKORY-SMOKED SAUSAGE AND CHEDDAR OMELET

Prep Time: 15 minutes
Cook Time: 30 minutes
Servings: 4
Wood Type: Hickory
Smoking Time: 20 minutes

Ingredients:
8 large eggs
1/2 cup milk
1 cup cheddar cheese, shredded
8 oz sausage, pre-smoked or cooked and diced
1/4 cup green bell pepper, diced
1/4 cup red onion, diced
1/4 cup tomatoes, diced
Salt and pepper to taste
2 tbsp unsalted butter or olive oil, for cooking
Fresh herbs (optional, for garnish)

Instructions:
- If using pre-smoked sausage, skip to step 2. Otherwise, preheat your electric smoker to 225°F with hickory wood chips. Place diced sausage in the smoker and smoke for about 20 minutes. Remove and set aside to cool.
- In a large mixing bowl, whisk together the eggs and milk until well combined. Stir in the smoked sausage, 3/4 cup of cheddar cheese, green bell pepper, red onion, and tomatoes. Season with salt and pepper.
- Heat a non-stick skillet or frying pan over medium heat. Add butter or olive oil to coat the bottom of the pan.
- Pour half of the egg mixture into the skillet, tilting to evenly cover the bottom. Cook for 3-4 minutes until the edges start to set. Using a spatula, gently lift the edges and tilt the pan to allow uncooked egg to flow to the bottom.
- Once the omelet is mostly set but still slightly runny on top, sprinkle an additional 1/4 cup of cheddar cheese over half of the omelet. Cook for another 1-2 minutes, then carefully flip and cook for 1 more minute to ensure it's fully set.
- Remove the omelet from the skillet and transfer to a plate. If desired, garnish with fresh herbs. Repeat the process with the remaining egg mixture to make the second omelet.

APPLEWOOD-SMOKED BACON AND EGGS BENEDICT

Prep Time: 20 minutes
Cook Time: 30 minutes
Servings: 4
Wood Type: Applewood
Smoking Time: 20 minutes

Ingredients
8 slices of thick-cut bacon
4 English muffins, halved
8 large eggs

1 cup distilled white vinegar (for poaching eggs)
1 teaspoon smoked paprika (for garnish)
Fresh chives, finely chopped (for garnish)
For the Hollandaise Sauce:
3 egg yolks
1 tablespoon lemon juice
1/2 cup unsalted butter, melted
1/4 teaspoon cayenne pepper
Salt, to taste

Instructions
- Set your electric smoker to 225°F and add applewood chips to the smoker box.
- Lay the bacon slices on a rack over a baking sheet or directly on the smoker racks, ensuring they are not touching. Smoke for 20 minutes. Once done, remove from the smoker and place on paper towels to drain any excess grease.
- Fill a small saucepan with about 3 inches of water and add the vinegar. Bring the water to a simmer. Crack an egg into a small bowl and gently slide it into the simmering water. Repeat with the remaining eggs. Poach for about 3 minutes. Use a slotted spoon to remove the eggs and drain on a kitchen towel.
- Split the English muffins and place them cut side up in the smoker for 5-7 minutes, or until they are lightly toasted.
- In a mixing bowl over a pot of simmering water (double boiler), whisk together the egg yolks and lemon juice until the mixture is thickened and doubled in volume. Slowly drizzle in the melted butter, continuing to whisk until the sauce is thickened. Remove from heat, and whisk in cayenne pepper and salt. Keep the sauce warm until ready to serve.
- Place two halves on each plate. Top each half with a slice of smoked bacon, followed by a poached egg. Spoon Hollandaise sauce over the eggs, and sprinkle with smoked paprika and chives for garnish.

SMOKED PORK BREAKFAST SAUSAGE PATTIES

Prep Time: 20 minutes
Cook Time: 1 hour 30 minutes
Servings: 4
Wood Type: Applewood
Smoking Time: 1 hour 30 minutes

Ingredients:
1 lb ground pork
2 teaspoons sage, finely chopped
1 teaspoon thyme, finely chopped
1 teaspoon brown sugar
1 teaspoon salt
1/2 teaspoon black pepper
1/4 teaspoon nutmeg
1/4 teaspoon cayenne pepper
1 garlic clove, minced
2 tablespoons ice water

Instructions:
- In a large mixing bowl, combine the ground pork with sage, thyme, brown sugar, salt, black pepper, nutmeg, cayenne pepper, and minced garlic. Mix thoroughly to ensure all the spices are evenly distributed throughout the pork.
- Drizzle the ice water over the pork mixture. The cold water helps to bind the fat and meat together, ensuring a juicy patty. Mix again until well combined.

- Lay a piece of parchment paper on a plate or tray. Using your hands, divide the pork mixture into 8 equal portions. Shape each portion into a patty. Place the formed patties on the parchment paper, making sure they don't touch each other.
- Preheat your electric smoker to 225°F. While the smoker is heating, soak your applewood chips in water for at least 30 minutes. This prevents them from burning too quickly and ensures a smooth, consistent smoke.
- Once the smoker has reached the desired temperature, drain the wood chips and add them to the smoker's wood chip compartment.
- Place the sausage patties in the smoker, ensuring there is enough space between them for the smoke to circulate.
- Close the smoker and let the patties smoke for approximately 1 hour 30 minutes, or until the internal temperature of the patties reaches 160°F. Use a thermometer to check the temperature.
- Once done, carefully remove the smoked pork breakfast sausage patties from the smoker and let them rest for a few minutes before serving. This allows the juices to redistribute, ensuring a moist and flavorful patty.
- Serve these delightful smoked pork breakfast sausage patties alongside your favorite breakfast items, such as eggs, pancakes, or toast, and enjoy the unique flavor that only smoking can impart.

MESQUITE-SMOKED HAM AND EGG BREAKFAST TACOS

Prep Time: 20 minutes
Cook Time: 1 hour 10 minutes
Servings: 4
Wood Type: Mesquite
Smoking Time: 30 minutes

Ingredients:
8 large eggs
1 tablespoon milk
1/2 teaspoon salt
1/4 teaspoon black pepper
1 cup diced ham (pre-cooked)
1 cup shredded cheddar cheese
8 small flour tortillas
1/4 cup chopped fresh cilantro
1/2 cup diced tomatoes
1/4 cup thinly sliced green onions
1 avocado, sliced
1/4 cup sour cream
1 lime, cut into wedges

Instructions:
- Preheat your electric smoker to 225°F. Add mesquite wood chips according to the manufacturer's instructions to get ready for smoking.
- Wrap the diced ham in aluminum foil and place it in the smoker. Smoke for 30 minutes to infuse the mesquite flavor. Once smoked, remove from the smoker and set aside.
- In a mixing bowl, whisk together eggs, milk, salt, and pepper until well combined.
- Heat a non-stick skillet over medium heat. Pour in the egg mixture and cook, stirring frequently, until the eggs are scrambled and just set. Remove from heat.
- Add the scrambled eggs to the smoked ham, folding gently to combine.
- Warm the flour tortillas on the skillet for about 30 seconds on each side or until soft and warm.
- Divide the ham and egg mixture evenly among the tortillas.
- Top each taco with shredded cheddar cheese, allowing the warmth of the eggs and ham to melt the cheese slightly.

- Sprinkle chopped cilantro, diced tomatoes, and sliced green onions over the top of each taco.
- Add slices of avocado and a dollop of sour cream to each taco.
- Serve with lime wedges on the side for squeezing over the tacos.

SWEET MAPLE SMOKED SAUSAGE LINKS

Prep Time: 15 minutes
Cook Time: 2 hours
Servings: 4
Wood Type: Maple
Smoking Time: 2 hours

Ingredients
1 lb. fresh sausage links (pork or chicken)
1/4 cup maple syrup
2 tbsp. brown sugar
1 tbsp. Dijon mustard
1 tsp. garlic powder
1/2 tsp. smoked paprika
Salt and pepper to taste
Olive oil for brushing

Instructions
- Preheat your electric smoker to 225°F and add maple wood chips to the designated tray.
- In a small bowl, mix together the maple syrup, brown sugar, Dijon mustard, garlic powder, smoked paprika, salt, and pepper to create a glaze.
- Lightly brush the sausage links with olive oil. This helps the smoke to adhere better and prevents the sausages from drying out.
- Arrange the sausages on the smoker racks, ensuring they're not touching to allow for even smoking.
- Place the sausages in the preheated smoker. Close the lid and smoke for about 2 hours.
- After the first hour, start basting the sausage links with the maple syrup glaze every 30 minutes to build up a sweet and caramelized exterior.
- Use a meat thermometer to check the internal temperature of the sausages. They are done when they reach an internal temperature of 160°F for pork or 165°F for chicken.
- Once cooked, carefully remove the sausages from the smoker using tongs and wrap them in aluminum foil. Let them rest for about 10 minutes. This step allows the juices to redistribute, making the sausages moist and flavorful.
- Unwrap the sausages and slice them into pieces if desired. Serve hot as a delightful appetizer or part of a main dish, accompanied by your favorite sides.

SMOKED BRISKET HASH WITH SUNNY-SIDE EGGS

Prep Time: 20 minutes
Cook Time: 2 hours (for the brisket, if not already prepared) + 30 minutes for the hash and eggs
Servings: 4
Wood Type: Hickory or Oak (for a robust, smoky flavor)
Smoking Time: 2 hours at 225°F (for the brisket, if not using leftovers)

Ingredients
1 lb smoked brisket, cooked and chopped into bite-sized pieces
3 large potatoes, diced
1 large onion, diced
1 red bell pepper, diced

2 cloves garlic, minced
4 large eggs
1 teaspoon smoked paprika
1/2 teaspoon ground cumin
Salt and pepper, to taste
2 tablespoons olive oil
Fresh parsley, chopped (for garnish)
Hot sauce (optional, for serving)

Instructions
- If you're starting with fresh brisket, season it generously with salt, pepper, and a touch of smoked paprika. Preheat your electric smoker to 225°F and add your choice of wood chips. Smoke the brisket until it reaches an internal temperature of 195°F, typically about 2 hours. Let it rest before chopping into bite-sized pieces. (Skip this step if you're using leftover smoked brisket.)
- While the brisket rests or if using leftovers, dice the potatoes, onion, and red bell pepper. Mince the garlic.
- Heat olive oil in a large skillet over medium-high heat. Add the diced potatoes and cook until they start to become tender and golden brown, about 10 minutes. Add the onions and bell peppers, cooking until softened, about 5 minutes. Stir in the garlic, smoked paprika, and ground cumin, cooking for another minute until fragrant.
- Mix in the chopped brisket with the vegetables, season with salt and pepper, and cook for an additional 5-10 minutes, until everything is well combined and heated through.
- In a separate pan, fry the eggs to your liking, aiming for sunny-side up to keep the yolks runny.
- Divide the hash among plates, top each with a sunny-side-up egg, garnish with fresh parsley, and if desired, a dash of hot sauce for an extra kick.
- Serve your Smoked Brisket Hash with Sunny-Side Eggs immediately, and revel in the symphony of flavors.

PECAN-SMOKED BREAKFAST SAUSAGE GRAVY OVER BISCUITS

Prep Time: 20 minutes
Cook Time: 30 minutes
Servings: 4
Wood Type: Pecan
Smoking Time: 1 hour

Ingredients:
1 pound breakfast sausage (pork or turkey)
2 tablespoons all-purpose flour
2 cups whole milk
1/2 teaspoon salt
1/2 teaspoon black pepper
1/2 teaspoon ground sage (optional)
8 biscuits, homemade or store-bought
1/4 cup chopped pecans (for garnish, optional)

Instructions:
- Preheat your electric smoker to 250°F. Add pecan wood chips to the smoker's wood chip tray. Let it come to temperature and start producing smoke.
- In a skillet over medium heat, cook the sausage until it's thoroughly browned and no longer pink, breaking it apart into crumbles as it cooks, about 10 minutes. Remove the sausage with a slotted spoon, leaving the drippings in the skillet.
- Over low heat, sprinkle the flour into the sausage drippings, whisking continuously to combine and cook the flour, about 1-2 minutes. Gradually whisk in the milk until smooth. Add salt, pepper, and ground sage

if using. Increase the heat to medium, and continue whisking until the gravy thickens, about 5-10 minutes.

- Transfer the sausage gravy into a heat-resistant dish that can go in your smoker. Place the dish in the smoker and smoke for 1 hour, stirring occasionally. This step infuses the gravy with a light, pecan-smoked flavor.
- While the gravy is smoking, bake or reheat the biscuits according to package instructions if store-bought, or prepare your homemade biscuits.
- Spoon the pecan-smoked sausage gravy over warm biscuits. Garnish with chopped pecans if desired. Serve immediately.

SMOKED ANDOUILLE AND SWEET POTATO SKILLET

Prep Time: 15 minutes
Cook Time: 1 hour
Servings: 4
Wood Type: Hickory
Smoking Time: 45 minutes

Ingredients
1 lb Andouille sausage, sliced into 1/2-inch pieces
2 large sweet potatoes, peeled and diced into 1/2-inch cubes
1 medium onion, diced
1 red bell pepper, diced
2 cloves garlic, minced
1 tsp smoked paprika
1/2 tsp ground cumin
1/4 tsp cayenne pepper (adjust to taste)
Salt and pepper to taste
2 tbsp olive oil
Fresh parsley, chopped (for garnish)

Instructions
- Preheat your electric smoker to 225°F with hickory wood chips ready for smoking. In a large mixing bowl, toss the sliced Andouille sausage with a little olive oil and a pinch of smoked paprika. Spread the sausage slices in a single layer on the smoker rack.
- Place the sausage in the smoker and smoke for 45 minutes to an hour, or until the edges start to slightly crisp up and the sausage has absorbed a good amount of smoke flavor.
- While the sausage is smoking, dice the sweet potatoes, onion, and red bell pepper into 1/2-inch pieces. Mince the garlic.
- Heat olive oil in a large skillet over medium heat. Add the onions and sweet potatoes, cooking for about 10 minutes, or until the sweet potatoes start to soften. Add the red bell pepper, garlic, smoked paprika, ground cumin, cayenne pepper, salt, and pepper. Stir well and sauté for another 5 minutes.
- Once the sausage is smoked and has a nice outer crust, remove it from the smoker. Increase the skillet heat to medium-high and add the sausage to the skillet with the vegetables. Mix well to combine.
- Cook the mixture for an additional 5-10 minutes, stirring occasionally, until the sweet potatoes are fully cooked through and slightly crispy on the edges.
- Remove the skillet from heat. Taste and adjust seasoning if necessary. Garnish with fresh parsley before serving. Enjoy your Smoked Andouille and Sweet Potato Skillet hot, perfect as a hearty main dish or a fulfilling side.

CHERRYWOOD-SMOKED BACON AND MUSHROOM FRITTATA

Prep Time: 20 minutes
Cook Time: 1 hour
Servings: 4
Wood Type: Cherrywood
Smoking Time: 30 minutes

Ingredients:
6 large eggs
1/2 cup heavy cream
4 slices thick-cut bacon, chopped
1 cup mushrooms, sliced
1 small onion, finely diced
1 cup cheddar cheese, shredded
1/4 cup green onions, chopped
Salt and pepper, to taste
1 tablespoon olive oil

Instructions:
- Preheat your electric smoker to 325°F and add cherrywood chips according to the manufacturer's instructions for creating a mild, sweet smoke.
- In a skillet over medium heat, add the olive oil, chopped bacon, and diced onion. Add the sliced mushrooms and cook for another 5-7 minutes until the mushrooms are soft and golden. Remove from heat and set aside.
- In a mixing bowl, whisk together the eggs, heavy cream, salt, and pepper until well combined.
- Add the cooked bacon, onion, and mushrooms to the skillet. Spread them out evenly. Pour the egg mixture over the bacon and vegetables. Sprinkle the top with shredded cheddar cheese and green onions.
- Place the skillet in the preheated smoker. Close the lid and smoke the frittata for about 30 minutes, or until the eggs are set and the top is lightly golden.
- Once the frittata is cooked through, carefully remove the skillet from the smoker. Let it cool for a few minutes before slicing into wedges.
- Serve the Cherrywood-Smoked Bacon and Mushroom Frittata warm, directly from the skillet. Enjoy the subtle sweetness of cherrywood smoke that complements the savory flavors of bacon and mushrooms.

SMOKED SALMON AND CREAM CHEESE SCRAMBLE

Prep Time: 15 minutes
Cook Time: 10 minutes
Servings: 4
Wood Type: Apple or Alder
Smoking Time: 1 hour for the salmon (if not using pre-smoked salmon)

Ingredients:
8 ounces of salmon (pre-smoked or fresh)
8 large eggs
4 ounces of cream cheese, cubed
2 tablespoons of fresh dill, chopped
1 tablespoon of unsalted butter
Salt and freshly ground black pepper, to taste
4 slices of whole-grain bread, toasted
1 tablespoon of capers (optional)
1 small red onion, thinly sliced (optional)

Instructions:

- Preheat your electric smoker to 225°F and fill it with apple or alder wood chips. Place the salmon on the smoker rack and smoke for about 1 hour or until the internal temperature reaches 145°F. Once done, remove from the smoker, let cool, and flake into pieces.
- Crack the eggs into a mixing bowl. Add salt and pepper to taste. Whisk until well beaten. Mix in the cream cheese cubes and chopped dill, reserving some dill for garnish.
- Heat a non-stick skillet over medium heat. Add the butter, swirling to coat the bottom of the pan. Once the butter is melted and foamy, pour in the egg mixture. Let it sit, without stirring, for about 1 minute until the bottom starts to set.
- With a spatula, gently stir the eggs from the edge to the center, forming large soft curds. Continue cooking until the eggs are softly set and slightly runny in places. Remove from the heat. The residual heat will continue cooking the eggs.
- Gently fold in the flaked smoked salmon into the eggs, being careful not to break the salmon pieces too much.
- Divide the scramble among plates. Top with remaining dill, capers, and red onion slices if using. Serve immediately with a side of toasted whole-grain bread.

ALDER-SMOKED TURKEY SAUSAGE AND VEGGIE QUICHE

Prep Time: 20 minutes
Cook Time: 1 hour
Servings: 4
Wood Type: Alder
Smoking Time: 30 minutes

Ingredients
For the Smoked Turkey Sausage and Veggies:
1/2 pound turkey sausage, casings removed
1 red bell pepper, diced
1 small zucchini, diced
1/2 yellow onion, diced
1 tablespoon olive oil
Salt and pepper, to taste
Alder wood chips, for smoking
For the Quiche:
1 store-bought pie crust, or homemade equivalent
6 large eggs
1 cup whole milk
1/2 cup grated cheddar cheese
1/2 cup grated mozzarella cheese
1/4 teaspoon salt
1/4 teaspoon black pepper
1/4 teaspoon smoked paprika
1 tablespoon fresh parsley, chopped (for garnish)

Instructions
- Preheat your electric smoker to 225°F and add alder wood chips according to the manufacturer's instructions.
- Prepare the turkey sausage and vegetables for smoking. In a bowl, combine the turkey sausage, diced red bell pepper, zucchini, and yellow onion. Drizzle with olive oil, season with salt and pepper, and toss to coat evenly.
- Spread the sausage and vegetable mixture in a single layer on a smoker-friendly tray or basket. Place in the smoker and smoke for 30 minutes, or until the sausage is fully cooked and the vegetables are tender and slightly charred. Remove from the smoker and let cool slightly. Increase the smoker temperature to 350°F for the quiche.

- While the sausage and veggies are smoking, prepare the quiche base. Roll out the pie crust and press it into a pie dish.
- In a large mixing bowl, whisk together the eggs, milk, cheddar cheese, mozzarella cheese, salt, black pepper, and smoked paprika until well combined.
- Chop the smoked sausage and veggies into smaller pieces if necessary, then spread them evenly over the bottom of the pie crust.
- Pour the egg and cheese mixture over the sausage and veggies in the pie crust, making sure the ingredients are evenly distributed.
- Place the quiche in the smoker (now preheated to 350°F) and smoke for approximately 30-35 minutes, or until the quiche is set and the crust is golden brown.
- Remove the quiche from the smoker and let it cool for a few minutes before slicing. Garnish with fresh parsley.
- Serve warm and enjoy the rich, smoky flavors of this alder-smoked turkey sausage and veggie quiche!

SMOKED PORK BELLY AND EGG BREAKFAST SANDWICH

Prep Time: 20 minutes
Cook Time: 3 hours
Servings: 4
Wood Type: Applewood
Smoking Time: 3 hours

Ingredients:
1 lb pork belly, skin removed
2 tbsp brown sugar
2 tbsp smoked paprika
1 tbsp coarse salt
1 tsp ground black pepper
1 tsp garlic powder
1 tsp onion powder
4 large eggs
4 slices of cheddar cheese
4 English muffins, split and toasted
Your choice of sauce (e.g., BBQ, hot sauce, or mayonnaise) for spreading
Optional toppings: sliced avocado, tomato, or arugula

Instructions:
- In a small bowl, mix together the brown sugar, smoked paprika, salt, black pepper, garlic powder, and onion powder. Rub this mixture all over the pork belly. Let it marinate in the fridge for at least 1 hour, or overnight for best flavor.
- Preheat your electric smoker to 225°F using applewood chips for a sweet, mild smoke flavor that complements the pork beautifully.
- Place the pork belly in the smoker and cook for about 3 hours, or until the internal temperature reaches 200°F. Once done, remove it from the smoker and let it rest for 10 minutes before slicing into thick pieces.
- While the pork belly rests, fry the eggs to your liking. For a runny yolk, cook for about 2-3 minutes per side over medium heat.
- Spread your chosen sauce on both halves of the toasted English muffins. Place a slice of cheddar cheese on the bottom halves, followed by a generous helping of sliced smoked pork belly, a fried egg, and any optional toppings you desire. Cap with the other half of the muffin.
- Serve the sandwiches immediately, ensuring the cheese melts beautifully over the warm pork belly and egg.

SMOKED CHORIZO AND EGG BREAKFAST BURRITOS

Prep Time: 15 minutes
Cook Time: 1 hour
Servings: 4
Wood Type: Apple
Smoking Time: 45 minutes

Ingredients:
8 large eggs
1/2 lb (about 225g) chorizo, casing removed and crumbled
4 large flour tortillas
1 cup shredded cheddar cheese
1 medium onion, finely chopped
1 green bell pepper, diced
2 tablespoons milk
1 tablespoon olive oil
1 teaspoon smoked paprika (for that extra smoky flavor)
Salt and pepper, to taste
Optional garnishes: sliced avocado, sour cream, salsa, chopped cilantro

Instructions:
- Set the smoker to 250°F and add apple wood chips for a sweet, mild smokiness that complements the chorizo and eggs perfectly.
- While the smoker preheats, heat the olive oil in a large skillet over medium heat. Add the chorizo, onion, and green bell pepper. Cook, stirring occasionally, until the chorizo is browned and the vegetables are soft, about 7-10 minutes. Remove from heat and set aside.
- In a bowl, whisk together the eggs, milk, smoked paprika, salt, and pepper. In the same skillet used for the chorizo (to soak up all those flavors), pour in the egg mixture. Cook over medium-low heat, stirring constantly, until the eggs are softly scrambled, about 3-4 minutes. Remove from heat.
- Add the scrambled eggs to the skillet with the chorizo mixture and stir to combine evenly.
- Lay out the flour tortillas and distribute the egg and chorizo mixture evenly among them. Sprinkle shredded cheese on top of the filling. If using any optional garnishes, add them now. Roll up the tortillas to form burritos.
- Transfer the assembled burritos to the smoker. Smoke for about 45 minutes, or until the tortillas are slightly crispy and the cheese has melted.
- Serve the smoked chorizo and egg breakfast burritos hot, with optional garnishes like sliced avocado, sour cream, salsa, and chopped cilantro on the side for an extra burst of flavor.

CEDAR-SMOKED EGG CUPS WITH SPINACH AND FETA

Prep Time: 15 minutes
Cook Time: 25 minutes
Servings: 4
Wood Type: Cedar
Smoking Time: 20 minutes

Ingredients:
8 large eggs
1 cup fresh spinach, finely chopped
1/2 cup feta cheese, crumbled
1/4 cup red bell pepper, finely diced
1/4 cup milk
1 tablespoon olive oil

1 teaspoon garlic powder
Salt and pepper to taste
Cooking spray (for greasing the muffin tins)
4 cedar wood planks, soaked in water for at least 1 hour before use

Instructions:
- Preheat your electric smoker to 350°F and place the soaked cedar planks inside to preheat as well.
- In a large bowl, whisk together the eggs, milk, garlic powder, salt, and pepper until well combined. Stir in the chopped spinach, crumbled feta cheese, and diced red bell pepper.
- Grease the muffin tins lightly with cooking spray. If using silicone muffin cups, place them on a baking sheet for easier handling.
- Fill the muffin tins with the egg mixture, dividing it evenly among the cups. Each cup should be filled about three-quarters of the way to allow room for the eggs to expand as they cook.
- Place the muffin tins (or baking sheet with silicone cups) directly on the cedar planks in the smoker. Close the smoker lid and smoke for about 20 minutes or until the eggs are set and lightly golden on top. The internal temperature of the egg cups should reach 160°F to ensure they are fully cooked.
- Let cool slightly before removing the egg cups from the muffin tins. Use a butter knife or a small spatula around the edges for easier removal if necessary.
- Serve immediately while warm, garnishing with additional feta cheese or fresh herbs if desired.

SMOKED GOUDA AND HAM BREAKFAST STRATA

Prep Time: 20 minutes
Cook Time: 1 hour 15 minutes
Servings: 4
Wood Type: Apple or Cherry
Smoking Time: 1 hour

Ingredients:
6 cups of day-old bread, cubed (preferably a hearty loaf like sourdough or ciabatta)
1 cup smoked gouda cheese, shredded
1 cup cooked ham, diced
1/2 cup green onions, thinly sliced
1/2 cup red bell pepper, diced
6 large eggs
2 cups whole milk
1 teaspoon mustard powder
1/2 teaspoon salt
1/4 teaspoon black pepper
Non-stick cooking spray or butter for greasing

Instructions:
- Preheat your electric smoker to 225°F, using apple or cherry wood chips for a mildly sweet smoke that complements the flavors of the gouda and ham.
- Grease a baking dish with non-stick cooking spray or butter. Layer half of the bread cubes at the bottom of the dish. Sprinkle half of the smoked gouda, ham, green onions, and red bell peppers evenly over the bread. Repeat with the remaining bread, gouda, ham, onions, and peppers.
- In a large bowl, whisk together the eggs, whole milk, mustard powder, salt, and black pepper until well combined. Pour this mixture evenly over the layered bread, ensuring all the bread is soaked. Gently press down with a spatula to ensure the bread absorbs the egg mixture.
- Allow the strata to sit for about 20 minutes at room temperature, so the bread fully absorbs the egg mixture. Alternatively, you can cover and refrigerate it overnight if you're preparing for breakfast the next day.

- Place the baking dish in the preheated smoker. Close the lid and smoke for approximately 1 hour or until the center is set and the top is golden brown. The exact time might vary based on the smoker and external conditions.
- Once cooked, remove the strata from the smoker and let it rest for 5-10 minutes. This rest period allows the strata to firm up, making it easier to slice.
- Cut the strata into squares and serve warm. For an extra touch, garnish with additional sliced green onions or a light drizzle of hollandaise sauce.

APPLEWOOD-SMOKED CHEDDAR CHEESE

Prep Time: 15 minutes
Cook Time: 2 hours
Servings: 4
Wood Type: Applewood
Smoking Time: 2 hours

Ingredients:
1 lb block of cheddar cheese (mild or sharp depending on preference)
2 cups applewood chips, soaked in water for at least 30 minutes

Instructions:
- Begin by pre-soaking your applewood chips in water for at least 30 minutes before you plan to start smoking. This helps in creating a smoother, more consistent smoke.
- Preheat your electric smoker to 90°F. It's crucial to maintain a low temperature as cheese melts quickly. If your smoker cannot go as low as 90°F, try to keep it under 100°F and consider placing a tray of ice inside the smoker to prevent the cheese from melting.
- While the smoker is preheating, take your block of cheddar cheese and cut it into ½ inch thick slices. This increases the surface area allowing more smoke to infuse the cheese.
- Once the smoker is at the desired temperature, drain your applewood chips and place them in the smoker's wood chip compartment. Place the slices of cheese on the smoker racks, ensuring there is some space between each slice for the smoke to circulate evenly.
- Close the smoker and let the cheese smoke for about 2 hours. Keep an eye on the temperature to ensure it remains low to avoid melting the cheese.
- After 2 hours, remove the cheese from the smoker and wrap each slice individually in parchment paper. Then, tightly wrap them in plastic wrap. This helps to lock in the smoky flavor as it settles.
- Place the wrapped cheese in the refrigerator and let it rest for at least 24 hours. For best results, waiting for 2 to 3 days allows the smoke flavor to fully permeate the cheese.
- Unwrap the cheese and let it come to room temperature before serving. This enhances both the flavor and texture of the smoked cheddar.
- Your applewood-smoked cheddar cheese is ready to be enjoyed. Serve it as part of a cheese platter, grate it over dishes, or enjoy it as is with some crackers and wine.

HICKORY-SMOKED SPICY ALMONDS

Prep Time: 10 minutes
Cook Time: 1 hour
Servings: 4
Wood Type: Hickory
Smoking Time: 1 hour

Ingredients
2 cups raw almonds
2 tablespoons olive oil
1 teaspoon smoked paprika
1/2 teaspoon garlic powder
1/2 teaspoon onion powder
1/4 teaspoon cayenne pepper (adjust to taste for spiciness)

1 teaspoon sea salt
1/2 teaspoon black pepper

Instructions
- Preheat your electric smoker to 250°F. While it's warming up, soak a handful of hickory wood chips in water for about 30 minutes to ensure they produce ample smoke without burning too quickly.
- In a large bowl, combine the raw almonds with olive oil, tossing them until they're well-coated. In a separate small bowl, mix together the smoked paprika, garlic powder, onion powder, cayenne pepper, sea salt, and black pepper. Sprinkle the spice mix over the almonds, tossing again until they're evenly coated with the seasoning.
- Drain the hickory wood chips and place them in the smoker's wood chip compartment. Spread the seasoned almonds in a single layer on a smoker rack or in a smoking basket. If your smoker doesn't come equipped with a basket designed for nuts or smaller items, you can use a sheet of aluminum foil with holes poked in it to allow smoke to circulate around the almonds.
- Place the almonds in the smoker and let them smoke for about 1 hour, stirring occasionally to ensure they smoke evenly. The goal is to infuse the almonds with a deep, smoky flavor while achieving a slightly dry and crunchy texture.
- Once smoked, remove the almonds from the smoker and let them cool completely. They will continue to crisp up as they cool down. Taste and adjust the seasoning with a bit more salt if necessary.

SMOKED GOUDA AND BACON-STUFFED MUSHROOMS

Prep Time: 20 minutes
Cook Time: 1 hour
Servings: 4
Wood Type: Hickory
Smoking Time: 45 minutes to 1 hour

Ingredients:
16 large cremini or button mushrooms, stems removed and reserved
4 slices thick-cut bacon, diced
1/2 cup smoked Gouda cheese, grated
1/4 cup cream cheese, softened
1/4 cup breadcrumbs
2 cloves garlic, minced
2 tablespoons fresh parsley, chopped
1 tablespoon olive oil, plus extra for brushing
Salt and freshly ground black pepper, to taste

Instructions:
- Gently clean the mushrooms with a damp cloth and remove the stems. Chop the stems finely and set aside. Brush the mushroom caps with olive oil and season with salt and pepper.
- In a skillet over medium heat, cook the diced bacon until crispy. Remove the bacon bits with a slotted spoon and set aside on a paper towel to drain. Keep the bacon grease in the skillet.
- In the same skillet with the bacon grease, add the chopped mushroom stems and sauté until they're soft, about 3-5 minutes. Add the minced garlic and cook for an additional minute until fragrant.
- In a mixing bowl, combine the sautéed mushroom stems and garlic, cooked bacon, smoked Gouda cheese, cream cheese, breadcrumbs, and parsley. Mix until well combined. Taste and adjust seasoning with salt and pepper.
- Spoon the filling into the mushroom caps, pressing slightly to compact the filling.
- Preheat your electric smoker to 225°F and add hickory wood chips according to the manufacturer's instructions.
- Place the stuffed mushrooms in the smoker. Smoke for 45 minutes to 1 hour, or until the mushrooms are tender and the filling is hot and bubbly.

- Remove the mushrooms from the smoker and let them rest for a few minutes before serving. They can be garnished with additional chopped parsley or a sprinkle of smoked paprika for an extra pop of flavor and color.

CHERRYWOOD-SMOKED PECANS WITH BROWN SUGAR GLAZE

Prep Time: 15 minutes
Cook Time: 1 hour
Servings: 4
Wood Type: Cherrywood
Smoking Time: 1 hour

Ingredients:
2 cups pecan halves
1/4 cup unsalted butter, melted
1/3 cup brown sugar, packed
1 teaspoon ground cinnamon
1/2 teaspoon salt
1/4 teaspoon ground cayenne pepper (optional for a spicy kick)
2 tablespoons pure maple syrup
1 teaspoon vanilla extract

Instructions:
- Set your electric smoker to 250°F and add cherrywood chips to the smoker box. Let it come to temperature and start producing a steady stream of smoke.
- Prepare the pecans: In a large bowl, combine the pecan halves with the melted butter, ensuring each pecan is well coated.
- In a separate bowl, mix together the brown sugar, cinnamon, salt, and cayenne pepper (if using). Sprinkle this mixture over the buttered pecans, tossing to coat evenly. Drizzle the maple syrup and vanilla extract over the coated pecans and stir until well combined.
- Spread the pecans in a single layer on a baking sheet or smoker tray lined with parchment paper or aluminum foil for easy cleanup. Place the tray in the preheated smoker.
- Smoke the pecans for about 1 hour, stirring occasionally to ensure even smoking and to prevent any pecans from burning. The pecans should be fragrant and slightly darkened.
- Remove the pecans from the smoker and let them cool completely. They will crisp up as they cool. Taste and adjust the seasoning if necessary, adding a little more salt or cayenne pepper to suit your preference.

SMOKED MOZZARELLA CAPRESE BITES

Prep Time: 15 minutes
Cook Time: 1 hour 30 minutes
Servings: 4
Wood Type: Cherry
Smoking Time: 1 hour

Ingredients:
8 oz fresh mozzarella cheese, cut into 1-inch cubes
2 medium ripe tomatoes, cut into 1-inch chunks
1/4 cup fresh basil leaves, plus more for garnish
2 tablespoons extra-virgin olive oil
1 tablespoon balsamic glaze
Salt and freshly ground black pepper, to taste

1/4 teaspoon garlic powder
Wooden skewers or toothpicks

Instructions:
- Soak the wooden skewers (if using) in water for at least 30 minutes before smoking to prevent them from burning.
- Thread a piece of mozzarella, a basil leaf, and a chunk of tomato onto each skewer or toothpick. Arrange the assembled bites on a plate or tray.
- Drizzle the olive oil evenly over the assembled bites. Then, season with salt, freshly ground black pepper, and a sprinkle of garlic powder.
- Preheat your electric smoker to 225°F using cherry wood for a subtly sweet smoke flavor that complements the mozzarella beautifully.
- Place the assembled bites directly on the smoker grates or in a smoker-safe dish. Smoke for 1 hour, or until the mozzarella has a nice smoky flavor and is slightly softened.
- Drizzle balsamic glaze over the smoked caprese bites just before serving. Garnish with additional fresh basil leaves for a burst of color and freshness.
- Serve immediately as a delightful appetizer or a light snack. These bites are best enjoyed fresh from the smoker to savor the warm, smoky cheese paired with the freshness of tomato and basil.

PECAN-SMOKED BRIE WITH CRANBERRY CHUTNEY

Prep Time: 20 minutes
Cook Time: 10 minutes (for chutney) + 1 hour (for Brie smoking)
Servings: 4
Wood Type: Pecan
Smoking Time: 1 hour

Ingredients:
For the Brie:
1 large wheel of Brie cheese (about 8 ounces)
1/4 cup pecan wood chips, soaked in water for at least 30 minutes
For the Cranberry Chutney:
1 cup fresh cranberries
1/2 cup orange juice
1/4 cup sugar
1 teaspoon orange zest
1/2 teaspoon grated ginger
1/4 teaspoon ground cinnamon
1/8 teaspoon ground cloves
A pinch of salt

Instructions:
- In a medium saucepan, combine cranberries, orange juice, sugar, orange zest, grated ginger, cinnamon, cloves, and a pinch of salt.
- Bring to a simmer over medium heat, stirring occasionally, until the cranberries burst and the mixture thickens, about 10 minutes.
- Remove from heat and let cool. The chutney will thicken further as it cools.
- Preheat your electric smoker to 250°F.
- Drain the soaked pecan wood chips and add them to the smoker's wood chip tray.
- Place the wheel of Brie in a small, shallow, smoker-safe dish.
- Once the smoker is preheated and producing smoke, place the dish with the Brie in the smoker.
- Smoke the Brie for about 1 hour, or until it's soft to the touch but not completely melted.
- Carefully remove the smoked Brie from the smoker and let it rest for a few minutes.

- Transfer the Brie to a serving platter and spoon the cranberry chutney over the top or alongside the cheese.
- Serve with crackers, sliced baguette, or apple slices for dipping.

SMOKED HAVARTI DILL CHEESE STICKS

Prep Time: 15 minutes
Cook Time: 1 hour 30 minutes
Servings: 4
Wood Type: Apple or Cherry
Smoking Time: 1 hour 30 minutes

Ingredients
1 lb Havarti cheese with dill, cut into ½ inch thick sticks
2 large eggs, beaten
1 cup all-purpose flour
1 cup panko breadcrumbs
1 tablespoon smoked paprika
1 teaspoon garlic powder
1 teaspoon onion powder
Salt and pepper to taste
Cooking spray (for the smoker rack)

Instructions
- Begin by cutting the Havarti dill cheese into sticks, ensuring they are about ½ inch thick. This size allows for a perfect balance of smoky flavor penetration and cheese integrity during the smoking process.
- Arrange three shallow dishes. Place the all-purpose flour seasoned with a pinch of salt and pepper in the first, beaten eggs in the second, and a mixture of panko breadcrumbs, smoked paprika, garlic powder, onion powder, salt, and pepper in the third.
- Coat each cheese stick in flour, tapping off the excess. Dip into the beaten egg. Finally, roll in the seasoned panko mixture, pressing gently to adhere the breadcrumbs to the cheese.
- Place the coated cheese sticks on a baking sheet lined with parchment paper. Freeze for about 30 minutes to firm up. This step is crucial as it helps maintain the cheese's shape during the smoking process.
- While the cheese chills, preheat your electric smoker to 225°F using apple or cherry wood chips. These wood types offer a sweet and mild smoke that complements the dill and Havarti beautifully.
- Spray the smoker rack with cooking spray to prevent sticking. Arrange the chilled cheese sticks on the rack, ensuring they are not touching. Smoke for 1 hour 30 minutes, or until the cheese is slightly softened and the exterior is golden.
- Allow the smoked Havarti dill cheese sticks to cool for a few minutes before serving. They are perfect on their own or with a side of raspberry preserves or honey for dipping.

MESQUITE-SMOKED CASHEWS WITH SEA SALT

Prep Time: 10 minutes
Cook Time: 1 hour
Servings: 4
Wood Type: Mesquite
Smoking Time: 1 hour

Ingredients:
2 cups raw cashews
1 tablespoon olive oil

1½ teaspoons sea salt, or to taste
Optional for a spicy twist: ½ teaspoon smoked paprika or chili powder

Instructions:
- Set your electric smoker to 250°F and add mesquite wood chips to the smoker's wood chip tray. Wait until the smoker reaches the desired temperature and begins to produce a steady stream of smoke.
- In a large bowl, combine the raw cashews with olive oil, ensuring each cashew is lightly coated. If you're adding a spicy twist, now's the time to sprinkle the smoked paprika or chili powder over the cashews and toss until evenly coated.
- Sprinkle the sea salt over the oiled and optionally spiced cashews, tossing again to ensure an even coating.
- Spread the cashews in a single layer on a smoker rack or in a smoker basket. If your smoker doesn't have a fine enough rack to hold the cashews, you can use a piece of aluminum foil with holes poked in it for ventilation, or a disposable aluminum tray with holes.
- Place the rack in the preheated smoker. Close the lid and smoke the cashews for about 1 hour. Stir the cashews every 20 minutes to ensure they smoke evenly and to check for doneness.
- Once the cashews have taken on a beautiful golden color and are fragrant with that irresistible mesquite smoke, remove them from the smoker. Let them cool for a few minutes before tasting; they will become crunchier as they cool. Adjust the sea salt if necessary, then serve as a delightful snack or appetizer.
- Any leftovers can be stored in an airtight container at room temperature for up to a week, making them a perfect make-ahead treat for gatherings or a savory snack on the go.

SMOKED PROVOLONE AND SUNDRIED TOMATO CROSTINI

Prep Time: 20 minutes
Cook Time: 10 minutes
Servings: 4
Wood Type: Apple
Smoking Time: 1 hour

Ingredients
1 baguette, sliced into 1/2-inch thick rounds
1/4 cup olive oil
1 garlic clove, halved
8 ounces Provolone cheese, sliced
1/2 cup sundried tomatoes in oil, drained and chopped
1/4 cup fresh basil leaves, chiffonade
Salt and freshly ground black pepper, to taste

Instructions
- Preheat your electric smoker to 225°F with apple wood chips. While the smoker is heating, brush both sides of the baguette slices lightly with olive oil. Rub one side of each slice with the cut side of the garlic clove for a hint of flavor.
- Place Provolone slices in a single layer on a piece of parchment paper or a smoking mat inside the smoker. Smoke for about 1 hour, or until the cheese has taken on a noticeable smoky flavor but hasn't melted. Remove the cheese from the smoker and set aside.
- Increase the smoker's temperature to 350°F. Arrange the oiled baguette slices on the smoker grate and toast for about 5 minutes per side, or until they are crispy and golden brown. Remove from the smoker and allow to cool slightly.
- On each baguette slice, lay a slice of smoked Provolone. Top with a spoonful of chopped sundried tomatoes and a sprinkle of basil. Season with salt and pepper to taste.
- Arrange the crostini on a serving platter. They can be served warm or at room temperature, allowing the smoky flavor of the Provolone to shine through, complemented by the tangy sundried tomatoes and fresh basil.

ALDER-SMOKED GOAT CHEESE WITH HONEY DRIZZLE

Prep Time: 10 minutes
Cook Time: 15 minutes
Servings: 4
Wood Type: Alder
Smoking Time: 2 hours

Ingredients:
8 oz goat cheese, log form (cut into 4 equal pieces)
2 tablespoons olive oil
1 teaspoon fresh thyme leaves, plus extra for garnish
1/2 teaspoon freshly ground black pepper
1/4 teaspoon sea salt
1/2 cup honey, for drizzling
Crackers or sliced baguette, for serving
Optional: Edible flowers for garnish

Instructions:
- Gently coat each piece of goat cheese with olive oil. Then, season with the thyme leaves, black pepper, and sea salt. Place the seasoned goat cheese on a smoking rack.
- Preheat your electric smoker to 225°F. While it's warming up, soak the alder wood chips in water for at least 30 minutes. This prevents them from igniting and promotes more smoke.
- Once the wood chips are soaked and the smoker is preheated, drain the chips and add them to the smoker's wood chip compartment. Place the rack with the goat cheese inside the smoker. Close the lid and smoke for 2 hours, or until the cheese is slightly softened and has a golden hue.
- After smoking, carefully remove the goat cheese from the smoker and let it rest for about 5 minutes. This allows the smoke flavor to settle and the cheese to firm up slightly, making it easier to serve.
- Transfer the smoked goat cheese to a serving plate. Drizzle generously with honey and garnish with additional thyme leaves and optional edible flowers.

HICKORY-SMOKED BLUE CHEESE AND WALNUT SPREAD

Prep Time: 15 minutes
Cook Time: 1 hour 30 minutes
Servings: 4
Wood Type: Hickory
Smoking Time: 1 hour

Ingredients:
8 oz (about 225g) cream cheese, softened
4 oz (about 115g) blue cheese, crumbled
1/2 cup walnuts, roughly chopped
2 tablespoons heavy cream (more if needed to adjust consistency)
1 clove garlic, minced
1 tablespoon fresh chives, finely chopped
Salt and pepper, to taste
Olive oil, for drizzling
Optional for serving: Crackers, sliced baguette, or fresh vegetable sticks

Instructions:

- In a medium bowl, combine the cream cheese, blue cheese, heavy cream, garlic, and chives. Mix well until the ingredients are fully incorporated and the mixture is smooth. If the mixture is too thick, add a bit more heavy cream to reach your desired consistency. Season with salt and pepper to taste.
- Transfer the cheese mixture into a shallow, heat-proof dish that is safe for use in your electric smoker. Smooth the top with a spatula, and sprinkle the chopped walnuts evenly over the surface. Drizzle a little olive oil over the top.
- Preheat your electric smoker to 225°F and add the hickory wood chips. Once the smoker is ready, place the dish with the cheese mixture inside. Close the lid and smoke for about 1 hour, or until the cheese has absorbed the hickory smoke flavor and the walnuts are lightly toasted.
- Carefully remove the dish from the smoker and let it cool for a few minutes. The spread can be served slightly warm or chilled, depending on your preference. If serving chilled, cover and refrigerate the spread for at least an hour to allow the flavors to meld together.
- Transfer the smoked blue cheese and walnut spread into a serving bowl. Drizzle with a bit more olive oil and sprinkle with additional chives for garnish if desired. Serve with your choice of crackers, sliced baguette, or fresh vegetable sticks for dipping.
- Invite your guests to dive into this creamy, smoky spread, perfect for an appetizer or a part of a cheese board.

CEDAR-SMOKED OLIVES AND FETA PLATTER

Prep Time: 10 minutes
Cook Time: 20 minutes
Servings: 4
Wood Type: Cedar
Smoking Time: 15 minutes

Ingredients:
1 cup mixed olives, drained
8 ounces feta cheese, cut into 1/2-inch cubes
1 tablespoon olive oil
1 teaspoon fresh rosemary, finely chopped
1 teaspoon fresh thyme, finely chopped
1/4 teaspoon red pepper flakes (optional for a spicy kick)
Zest of 1 lemon
2 cedar planks, soaked in water for at least 1 hour before use

Instructions:
- Preheat your electric smoker to 225°F with the lid closed. While the smoker preheats, soak the cedar planks in water to prevent them from catching fire.
- In a medium bowl, combine the mixed olives, cubed feta cheese, olive oil, chopped rosemary, thyme, red pepper flakes (if using), and lemon zest. Gently toss to ensure the olives and feta are well coated with the oil and herbs.
- Once the cedar planks are soaked and the smoker is preheated, arrange the olive and feta mixture evenly on the planks. Make sure the pieces are not overcrowded to allow the smoke to circulate freely.
- Place the cedar planks in the smoker. Close the lid and smoke for 15 minutes. The goal is to infuse the olives and feta with a gentle cedar smoke flavor without melting the cheese completely.
- After smoking, carefully remove the cedar planks from the smoker. Allow the olives and feta to cool for a couple of minutes before serving. This dish is best enjoyed slightly warm, allowing the smoky flavors to shine.

SMOKED PEPPER JACK AND JALAPEÑO POPPERS

Prep Time: 20 minutes

Cook Time: 2 to 3 hours
Servings: 4
Wood Type: Apple or Hickory
Smoking Time: 2 to 3 hours at 225°F

Ingredients:
8 large jalapeños, halved lengthwise and deseeded
8 oz (225 g) cream cheese, softened
1 cup (100 g) shredded Pepper Jack cheese
¼ cup (60 ml) green onions, finely chopped
1 teaspoon (5 ml) garlic powder
1 teaspoon (5 ml) smoked paprika
8 slices of thin bacon, cut in half
Toothpicks, for securing bacon
Salt and pepper, to taste

Instructions:
- Begin by slicing the jalapeños in half lengthwise. Using a spoon, scrape out the seeds and membranes, creating a hollow space for the filling. This step is crucial for perfect poppers, so take your time.
- In a medium bowl, combine the softened cream cheese, shredded Pepper Jack cheese, finely chopped green onions, garlic powder, and smoked paprika. Season with salt and pepper to taste. Mix until well combined.
- Spoon the cheese mixture into each jalapeño. The blend of cream cheese and Pepper Jack will ensure a creamy yet spicy popper.
- Carefully wrap a half slice of bacon around each stuffed jalapeño. Secure the bacon with a toothpick, ensuring it stays in place during the smoking process. The bacon not only adds flavor but also keeps the filling from melting out.
- Preheat your electric smoker to 225°F, using apple or hickory wood chips for a sweet or robust smoke flavor, respectively.
- Place the jalapeño poppers directly on the smoker grates. Smoke for 2 to 3 hours, or until the bacon is crispy and the peppers are tender. The low and slow smoke infuses the poppers with a delectable smoky flavor, complementing the spicy and cheesy filling.
- Remove the poppers from the smoker and let them rest for a few minutes. Serve warm for a melt-in-your-mouth experience that's bursting with flavor.

APPLEWOOD-SMOKED STUFFED CHERRY PEPPERS

Prep Time: 20 minutes
Cook Time: 2 hours
Servings: 4
Wood Type: Applewood
Smoking Time: 1.5 hours

Ingredients:
16 large cherry peppers
8 oz cream cheese, softened
1 cup sharp cheddar cheese, grated
4 oz cooked ham, finely chopped
2 cloves garlic, minced
1/4 cup green onions, finely sliced
1 tsp smoked paprika
Salt and pepper, to taste
Olive oil, for drizzling
2 tbsp fresh parsley, chopped, for garnish

Instructions:
- Slice off the tops of the cherry peppers and carefully remove the seeds and membranes with a small spoon. Rinse the peppers and pat them dry with paper towels.
- In a mixing bowl, combine the softened cream cheese, sharp cheddar cheese, finely chopped ham, minced garlic, green onions, and smoked paprika. Season with salt and pepper to taste. Mix until all ingredients are well incorporated.
- Carefully spoon the cheese mixture into each cherry pepper, filling them generously. Once all the peppers are stuffed, lightly drizzle them with olive oil.
- Preheat your electric smoker to 225°F and add applewood chips according to the manufacturer's instructions.
- Place the stuffed cherry peppers on a smoking rack, making sure they are not touching each other for even smoke circulation. Close the smoker and smoke the peppers for approximately 1.5 hours, or until they are tender and the filling is slightly golden.
- Remove the peppers from the smoker and allow them to cool slightly. Garnish with chopped fresh parsley before serving.
- Serve these Applewood-Smoked Stuffed Cherry Peppers as a delightful appetizer or side dish that combines the gentle sweetness of applewood smoke with the vibrant flavors of the stuffing, creating a memorable dish that's sure to impress.

SMOKED PARMESAN AND GARLIC BREAD BITES

Prep Time: 15 minutes
Cook Time: 1 hour
Servings: 4
Wood Type: Apple
Smoking Time: 45 minutes to 1 hour

Ingredients
1 large baguette, cut into 1-inch cubes
4 tablespoons unsalted butter, melted
2 cloves garlic, minced
½ cup grated Parmesan cheese
1 teaspoon dried oregano
1 teaspoon dried basil
½ teaspoon salt
¼ teaspoon black pepper
Olive oil spray (for the smoker rack)
Fresh parsley, chopped (for garnish)

Instructions
- In a large bowl, toss the baguette cubes with the melted butter, minced garlic, grated Parmesan, dried oregano, dried basil, salt, and black pepper until well coated.
- Preheat your electric smoker to 225°F with the lid closed. It's crucial to let it come to temperature before adding the wood chips. Fill the wood chip tray with apple wood chips, as apple wood imparts a slightly sweet and mild smokiness that complements the Parmesan and garlic flavors.
- Lightly spray the smoker rack with olive oil spray to prevent sticking. Spread the seasoned bread cubes in a single layer on the rack, ensuring they're not touching too much to allow for even smoke circulation.
- Place the rack in the smoker and close the lid. Smoke the bread bites for 45 minutes to 1 hour, or until they are crispy and golden brown. The exact time might vary depending on your smoker, so it's good to check them after 45 minutes.
- The bread bites are done when they are crispy on the outside and still slightly tender on the inside. If you prefer extra crispy bites, you can extend the smoking time by a few minutes, keeping a close eye on them to prevent burning.

- Once done, carefully remove the bread bites from the smoker and let them cool for a few minutes. Transfer to a serving platter, sprinkle with fresh chopped parsley for a pop of color and freshness, and serve immediately.

MESQUITE-SMOKED CHORIZO AND CHEESE DIP

Prep Time: 15 minutes
Cook Time: 1 hour
Servings: 4
Wood Type: Mesquite
Smoking Time: 45 minutes to 1 hour

Ingredients:
1 lb (450g) chorizo sausage, casing removed and crumbled
1 large onion, finely chopped
1 red bell pepper, finely chopped
2 cloves garlic, minced
1 cup (240ml) beer (preferably a light lager)
1 lb (450g) cream cheese, softened
2 cups (200g) shredded sharp cheddar cheese
1 cup (100g) shredded Monterey Jack cheese
1 teaspoon smoked paprika
1/2 teaspoon ground cumin
Salt and black pepper, to taste
Chopped green onions and cilantro, for garnish
Tortilla chips, for serving

Instructions:
- Preheat your electric smoker to 225°F and add mesquite wood chips to the smoker box.
- In a medium skillet over medium heat, cook the crumbled chorizo until it starts to brown, about 5-7 minutes. Add the chopped onion and red bell pepper, cooking until softened, about 5 minutes. Stir in the minced garlic and cook for another minute until fragrant.
- Pour the beer into the skillet with the chorizo mixture, scraping up any browned bits from the bottom of the skillet. Allow the mixture to simmer and reduce slightly, about 5 minutes. Remove from heat.
- In a large bowl, combine the softened cream cheese, shredded sharp cheddar cheese, Monterey Jack cheese, smoked paprika, and ground cumin. Season with salt and black pepper to taste. Mix until well combined.
- Fold the chorizo mixture into the cheese mixture until evenly distributed.
- Transfer the dip mixture into a cast-iron skillet or a smoker-safe dish. Smooth the top with a spatula.
- Place the skillet in the preheated smoker. Close the lid and smoke the dip for 45 minutes to 1 hour, or until it's bubbly and the top starts to brown slightly.
- Carefully remove the skillet from the smoker. Garnish the dip with chopped green onions and cilantro. Serve warm with tortilla chips for dipping.

CHERRYWOOD-SMOKED MARCONA ALMONDS

Prep Time: 10 minutes
Cook Time: 1 hour
Servings: 4
Wood Type: Cherrywood
Smoking Time: 1 hour

Ingredients:

2 cups Marcona almonds, raw and unsalted
1 tablespoon olive oil
1 teaspoon fine sea salt, or to taste
1/2 teaspoon smoked paprika
1/4 teaspoon garlic powder
1/4 teaspoon onion powder
Optional: 1/8 teaspoon cayenne pepper, for a bit of heat

Instructions:
- Preheat your electric smoker to 250°F and add cherrywood chips according to the manufacturer's instructions for smoke generation.
- In a medium bowl, combine the Marcona almonds and olive oil. Toss until the almonds are evenly coated. In a small bowl, mix together the sea salt, smoked paprika, garlic powder, onion powder, and cayenne pepper if using. Sprinkle the spice mix over the almonds and toss again to ensure they are well-coated with the seasoning.
- Spread the seasoned almonds in a single layer on a smoker rack or in a smoking basket. If your smoker doesn't come with a suitable rack or basket for small items, you can use a disposable aluminum tray with holes poked in it for air circulation.
- Place the almonds in the preheated smoker. Close the lid and smoke for 1 hour, stirring occasionally, until the almonds are golden and aromatic.
- Remove the almonds from the smoker and let them cool on a wire rack or cool plate. They will continue to crisp up as they cool.
- Once cooled, taste and adjust the seasoning with a little more salt if needed. Serve the almonds as a snack on their own or as a crunchy addition to salads or cheese boards.

SMOKED GRUYÈRE AND MUSHROOM TARTLETS

Prep Time: 30 minutes
Cook Time: 45 minutes
Servings: 4
Wood Type: Apple
Smoking Time: 1 hour

Ingredients
1 sheet of puff pastry, thawed
1 tablespoon olive oil
1 small onion, finely chopped
2 garlic cloves, minced
8 ounces cremini mushrooms, thinly sliced
Salt and freshly ground black pepper, to taste
1 teaspoon fresh thyme leaves, plus more for garnish
1/4 cup white wine (optional)
1/2 cup heavy cream
1 cup grated Gruyère cheese
1 egg, beaten for egg wash

Instructions
- Set your electric smoker to 225°F using apple wood chips to infuse a mild, sweet flavor that complements the Gruyère and mushrooms.
- Roll out the puff pastry on a lightly floured surface. Cut into 4-inch squares or circles, depending on your tartlet pans. Press the pastry into 4 tartlet pans with removable bottoms, trimming any excess. Prick the bottom with a fork. Chill in the refrigerator for about 15 minutes.
- While the puff pastry chills, heat olive oil in a skillet over medium heat. Add onion and garlic, sautéing until soft and translucent, about 5 minutes. Add mushrooms, salt, pepper, and thyme. Cook until the

mushrooms are soft and browned, about 8 minutes. Deglaze the pan with white wine if using, allowing it to evaporate. Stir in heavy cream and cook for another 2 minutes until slightly thickened. Remove from heat and let cool slightly. Stir in the grated Gruyère cheese.

- Spoon the mushroom and cheese mixture into the chilled tartlet shells. Brush the edges of the pastry with the beaten egg.
- Place the tartlets in the smoker. Smoke for about 1 hour, or until the pastry is golden and puffed, and the filling is bubbly and aromatic.

PECAN-SMOKED MANCHEGO WITH QUINCE PASTE

Prep Time: 15 minutes
Cook Time: 1 hour
Servings: 4
Wood Type: Pecan
Smoking Time: 1 hour

Ingredients:
1 large wedge Manchego cheese (approximately 8 ounces)
1/4 cup olive oil
1 tablespoon fresh rosemary leaves, finely chopped
1 clove garlic, minced
Freshly ground black pepper, to taste
1 cup quince paste (membrillo), sliced into thin wedges
Crackers or sliced baguette, for serving

Instructions:
- Begin by patting the Manchego cheese dry with paper towels. In a small bowl, mix together the olive oil, finely chopped rosemary, minced garlic, and a generous grind of black pepper. Rub this mixture all over the Manchego cheese, ensuring it's well coated.
- Preheat your electric smoker to 225°F, setting it up for indirect smoking. While it's heating, soak your pecan wood chips in water for at least 30 minutes. This prevents them from burning too quickly and imparts a gentle, smoky flavor to the cheese.
- Once the smoker is ready and the wood chips are drained, place the Manchego cheese on the smoker grate. Close the lid and smoke the cheese for about 1 hour. Keep an eye on the cheese; you want it to soften slightly and take on a golden hue, not melt completely.
- After smoking, allow the cheese to rest for about 5 minutes. Then, transfer it to a serving platter. Slice the smoked Manchego into wedges or thick slices and serve alongside the quince paste and crackers or slices of baguette.
- Encourage your guests to spread the quince paste on a cracker or slice of baguette and top with a slice of the smoked Manchego. The combination of the nutty, smoky cheese with the sweet, tangy quince paste is a match made in culinary heaven.

HICKORY-SMOKED SALMON AND CREAM CHEESE SPREAD

Prep Time: 20 minutes
Cook Time: 1 hour
Servings: 4
Wood Type: Hickory
Smoking Time: 1 hour

Ingredients:
1 pound fresh salmon fillet, skin on
1 tablespoon olive oil

1 teaspoon salt
1/2 teaspoon freshly ground black pepper
1/2 teaspoon garlic powder
8 ounces cream cheese, softened
2 tablespoons fresh dill, chopped
1 tablespoon lemon juice
2 teaspoons capers, drained and chopped
1/4 teaspoon smoked paprika (optional for extra smoky flavor)
Crackers or sliced baguette, for serving

Instructions:
- Preheat your electric smoker to 225°F and add hickory wood chips according to the manufacturer's instructions for smoke generation.
- Prepare the salmon by rinsing under cold water and patting dry with paper towels. Drizzle olive oil over the salmon and season evenly with salt, black pepper, and garlic powder.
- Place the salmon, skin-side down, directly on the smoker rack. Close the lid and smoke for 1 hour, or until the internal temperature of the salmon reaches 145°F and the flesh flakes easily with a fork.
- Once smoked, remove the salmon from the smoker and let it cool. Once cool enough to handle, flake the salmon into small pieces, discarding the skin.
- In a medium bowl, combine the flaked salmon, softened cream cheese, chopped dill, lemon juice, capers, and smoked paprika (if using). Mix until well combined but still slightly chunky for texture.
- Taste and adjust seasoning, adding more salt, pepper, or lemon juice if needed.
- Serve the smoked salmon and cream cheese spread with crackers or sliced baguette. It's also delightful spread on cucumber slices or stuffed into cherry tomatoes for a light appetizer.

MAIN COURSES: SIGNATURE SMOKED BRISKET, PULLED PORK, AND MORE

CLASSIC HICKORY-SMOKED BEEF BRISKET

Prep Time: 30 minutes
Cook Time: 8 to 10 hours
Servings: 4
Wood Type: Hickory
Smoking Time: 8 to 10 hours

Ingredients:
4 lbs beef brisket, flat cut
2 tablespoons kosher salt
2 tablespoons black pepper, freshly ground
1 tablespoon smoked paprika
1 tablespoon garlic powder
1 tablespoon onion powder
2 teaspoons brown sugar
1 teaspoon cayenne pepper (optional for heat)
1/2 cup apple cider vinegar (for spritzing)
Hickory wood chips for smoking

Instructions:
- Begin by patting the beef brisket dry with paper towels. Mix together the kosher salt, black pepper, smoked paprika, garlic powder, onion powder, brown sugar, and cayenne pepper in a small bowl. Rub this seasoning blend all over the brisket, ensuring every inch is covered. Let the brisket sit at room temperature for about 30 minutes to absorb the flavors.
- While the brisket is resting, preheat your electric smoker to 225°F. Load it with hickory wood chips, but don't overfill. Aim for a steady smoke without overwhelming the brisket with too much at once.
- Place the brisket fat-side up in the smoker. Close the lid and smoke for about 8 to 10 hours, maintaining a smoker temperature of 225°F. Spritz the brisket with apple cider vinegar every hour to keep it moist and enhance the flavor.
- The brisket is done when an instant-read thermometer inserted into the thickest part of the meat reads 195°F to 205°F. This range ensures the brisket is tender and juicy.
- Once the brisket reaches the desired internal temperature, carefully remove it from the smoker. Wrap it in butcher paper and let it rest for at least 1 hour.
- After resting, slice the brisket against the grain into thin slices. Serve warm with your favorite sides like coleslaw, baked beans, or cornbread.

APPLEWOOD-SMOKED PULLED PORK WITH CAROLINA VINEGAR SAUCE

Prep Time: 30 minutes
Cook Time: 8 hours
Servings: 4
Wood Type: Applewood
Smoking Time: 7 to 8 hours

Ingredients

For the Pulled Pork:
4 lbs pork shoulder (also known as pork butt)
2 tablespoons brown sugar
1 tablespoon paprika
1 tablespoon kosher salt
1 teaspoon ground black pepper
1 teaspoon garlic powder
1 teaspoon onion powder
1/2 teaspoon cayenne pepper (adjust to taste)
1/4 cup apple cider vinegar
1/4 cup water
Applewood chips, soaked in water for at least 30 minutes
For the Carolina Vinegar Sauce:
1 cup apple cider vinegar
1 tablespoon brown sugar
1 teaspoon crushed red pepper flakes
1 teaspoon kosher salt
1/2 teaspoon ground black pepper
2 tablespoons ketchup (optional, for a slightly thicker, sweeter sauce)

Instructions
- In a small bowl, combine brown sugar, paprika, kosher salt, ground black pepper, garlic powder, onion powder, and cayenne pepper to create the rub. Apply the rub generously over the entire surface of the pork shoulder.
- Preheat your electric smoker to 225°F. Make sure your applewood chips are soaked and drained before using.
- Place the pork shoulder in the smoker. Mix the apple cider vinegar and water, and spray or brush this mixture onto the pork every hour to keep it moist. Smoke the pork until it reaches an internal temperature of 195°F to 205°F, about 7 to 8 hours. Add applewood chips as needed to maintain smoke.
- Once the pork has reached the desired internal temperature, remove it from the smoker and let it rest.
- While the pork rests, combine apple cider vinegar, brown sugar, crushed red pepper flakes, kosher salt, black pepper, and ketchup (if using) in a small saucepan. Bring to a simmer over medium heat, stirring until the sugar and salt have dissolved. Remove from heat and let cool to room temperature.
- After resting, shred the pork using two forks or your hands, discarding any excess fat or gristle.
- Toss the pulled pork with some of the Carolina Vinegar Sauce, serving extra sauce on the side. Serve the pulled pork on its own or piled high on soft buns with coleslaw and your favorite sides.

MESQUITE-SMOKED TURKEY BREAST WITH HERB BUTTER

Prep Time: 20 minutes
Cook Time: 3 to 4 hours
Servings: 4
Wood Type: Mesquite
Smoking Time: 3 to 4 hours

Ingredients:
2 lbs turkey breast, boneless and skin-on
2 tablespoons olive oil
1/4 cup unsalted butter, softened
2 garlic cloves, minced
1 tablespoon fresh rosemary, finely chopped
1 tablespoon fresh thyme, finely chopped
1 tablespoon fresh sage, finely chopped
1 teaspoon salt

1/2 teaspoon black pepper
Mesquite wood chips, for smoking

Instructions:
- Begin by preheating your electric smoker to 225°F. Soak mesquite wood chips in water for at least 30 minutes before you plan to smoke.
- In a small bowl, combine the softened butter with minced garlic, rosemary, thyme, sage, salt, and pepper. Mix well.
- Rinse the turkey breast and pat dry with paper towels. Using your fingers, gently loosen the skin from the meat without completely detaching it. Spread half of the herb butter mixture under the skin, distributing it evenly over the meat. Rub the remaining herb butter mixture on the outside of the turkey breast, covering all sides. Drizzle olive oil over the turkey breast and ensure it's evenly coated.
- Once the smoker reaches the desired temperature, drain the wood chips and add them to the smoker's wood chip compartment. Place the turkey breast on the smoker rack, ensuring it's positioned in the center.
- Close the smoker lid and smoke the turkey breast for 3 to 4 hours, or until the internal temperature reaches 165°F. It's advisable to check the temperature at the 3-hour mark using a meat thermometer inserted into the thickest part of the breast.
- Once the turkey breast reaches the correct internal temperature, remove it from the smoker and let it rest for 10 minutes. This allows the juices to redistribute throughout the meat, ensuring it's moist and flavorful.
- After resting, slice the turkey breast against the grain into thick slices. Serve immediately.

CHERRYWOOD-SMOKED LAMB SHOULDER WITH ROSEMARY

Prep Time: 30 minutes
Cook Time: 4 to 5 hours
Servings: 4
Wood Type: Cherrywood
Smoking Time: 4 to 5 hours at 225°F

Ingredients:
3 lbs lamb shoulder, bone-in
2 tablespoons olive oil
4 cloves garlic, minced
2 tablespoons fresh rosemary, finely chopped
1 tablespoon kosher salt
1 teaspoon freshly ground black pepper
1 teaspoon smoked paprika
1/2 teaspoon onion powder
1/4 cup apple cider vinegar
1/4 cup water
Cherrywood chips, for smoking

Instructions:
- In a small bowl, mix together the olive oil, minced garlic, chopped rosemary, kosher salt, black pepper, smoked paprika, and onion powder to create a rub. Pat the lamb shoulder dry with paper towels.
- Apply the rub generously over the entire surface of the lamb shoulder, massaging it into the meat. Let the lamb marinate for at least 1 hour in the refrigerator, or for best results, overnight.
- Preheat your electric smoker to 225°F and add the cherrywood chips to the smoker's wood chip container.
- Remove the lamb from the refrigerator and let it come to room temperature, about 30 minutes. Place the lamb shoulder in the smoker on a rack over a drip pan. Mix the apple cider vinegar and water, and add it to the drip pan to help maintain moisture during the smoking process.

- Smoke the lamb shoulder for 4 to 5 hours, or until the internal temperature reaches 195°F for beautifully tender meat. If desired, wrap the lamb in aluminum foil after the first 3 hours to prevent the exterior from getting too dark and to retain moisture.
- Once done, remove the lamb shoulder from the smoker and let it rest for 20 to 30 minutes. This allows the juices to redistribute throughout the meat, ensuring it's moist and flavorful.
- Carve the lamb shoulder against the grain into thick slices. Serve with a side of roasted vegetables, or your choice of sides, and enjoy the succulent, smoky flavors infused by the cherrywood and rosemary.

SMOKED PORK RIBS WITH SWEET AND SPICY BBQ SAUCE

Prep Time: 15 minutes
Cook Time: 6 hours
Servings: 4
Wood Type: Apple or Hickory
Smoking Time: 6 hours

Ingredients:
For the Ribs:
2 racks of pork ribs (about 4-5 lbs)
2 tablespoons brown sugar
1 tablespoon paprika
1 tablespoon garlic powder
1 tablespoon onion powder
1 teaspoon cayenne pepper (adjust to taste for spiciness)
1 teaspoon black pepper
1 teaspoon salt
For the Sweet and Spicy BBQ Sauce:
1 cup ketchup
1/2 cup apple cider vinegar
1/2 cup brown sugar
1/4 cup honey
1 tablespoon Worcestershire sauce
1 tablespoon hot sauce (adjust to taste)
1 teaspoon garlic powder
1 teaspoon onion powder
Salt and pepper to taste

Instructions:
- Remove the membrane from the back of the ribs for better flavor absorption.
- In a bowl, mix brown sugar, paprika, garlic powder, onion powder, cayenne pepper, black pepper, and salt. Rub this mixture all over the ribs, ensuring both sides are well-coated.
- Preheat your electric smoker to 225°F. Use wood chips of your choice, either apple for a sweeter, milder smoke or hickory for a more robust flavor.
- Place the ribs in the smoker. Smoke for about 6 hours, or until the meat is tender and pulls away from the bones. If you prefer your ribs to have a bit of a bark, you can increase the temperature to 250°F during the last hour of cooking.
- In a saucepan over medium heat, combine ketchup, apple cider vinegar, brown sugar, honey, Worcestershire sauce, hot sauce, garlic powder, and onion powder. Season with salt and pepper to taste.
- Bring the sauce to a simmer, stirring occasionally, until it thickens and the flavors meld together, about 15-20 minutes. Adjust the sweetness or spiciness according to your preference by adding more honey or hot sauce.
- In the last 30 minutes of smoking, generously brush the ribs with the sweet and spicy BBQ sauce, allowing it to caramelize slightly.

- Once done, remove the ribs from the smoker and let them rest for about 10 minutes before slicing. Serve with additional BBQ sauce on the side for those who prefer a little extra flavor.

ALDER-SMOKED CORNISH HENS WITH LEMON AND THYME

Prep Time: 30 minutes
Cook Time: 1 hour and 30 minutes
Servings: 4
Wood Type: Alder
Smoking Time: 1 hour and 30 minutes

Ingredients
4 Cornish hens (approximately 1 to 1.5 pounds each)
2 lemons, quartered
4 sprigs of fresh thyme
2 tablespoons olive oil
4 cloves garlic, minced
Salt, to taste
Freshly ground black pepper, to taste
1 teaspoon smoked paprika
Additional thyme sprigs and lemon slices for garnishing

Instructions
- Begin by rinsing the Cornish hens under cold water and patting them dry with paper towels. Ensure they're completely dry to help the smoke adhere better.
- Rub each hen with olive oil. Then, season generously inside and out with salt, freshly ground black pepper, and smoked paprika. Stuff the cavity of each hen with a quarter of a lemon and a sprig of thyme. Tie the legs together with kitchen twine and tuck the wing tips under the body to prevent them from burning.
- Preheat your electric smoker to 225°F. While it heats, let the seasoned hens sit at room temperature. This step ensures they cook evenly.
- Once your smoker reaches the desired temperature, place the hens breast side up on the smoker rack. Add alder wood chips to the smoker according to the manufacturer's instructions. Close the lid and smoke for about 1 hour and 30 minutes, or until the internal temperature reaches 165°F when checked with a meat thermometer inserted into the thickest part of the thigh, not touching bone.
- Remove the hens from the smoker and let them rest for about 10 minutes. This allows the juices to redistribute, ensuring each bite is moist and flavorful.
- Garnish the hens with additional thyme sprigs and lemon slices. Carve and serve immediately.

SMOKED BEEF SHORT RIBS WITH COFFEE RUB

Prep Time: 20 minutes
Cook Time: 6 hours
Servings: 4
Wood Type: Hickory or Oak
Smoking Time: 6 hours

Ingredients:
4 lbs beef short ribs, bone-in
2 tablespoons ground coffee (medium roast)
1 tablespoon brown sugar
1 tablespoon paprika
1 tablespoon coarse salt

1 teaspoon black pepper
1 teaspoon garlic powder
1 teaspoon onion powder
1/2 teaspoon cayenne pepper (adjust to taste)
1/4 cup olive oil

Instructions:
- In a small bowl, combine the ground coffee, brown sugar, paprika, coarse salt, black pepper, garlic powder, onion powder, and cayenne pepper. Mix well to create the rub.
- Rinse the beef short ribs under cold water and pat them dry with paper towels. Trim any excess fat if desired. Brush each rib generously with olive oil.
- Liberally apply the coffee rub mixture to all sides of the beef short ribs, pressing gently to adhere. Let the ribs sit at room temperature for about 15 minutes to allow the rub to penetrate the meat.
- Preheat your electric smoker to 225°F. While the smoker is heating, soak your wood chips (hickory or oak) in water for about 15 minutes, then drain.
- Place the prepared ribs in the smoker. Add the soaked wood chips to the smoker's wood chip compartment. Close the lid and smoke the ribs for about 6 hours or until the meat is tender and pulls away from the bone easily. The internal temperature should reach around 200°F for optimal tenderness.
- Once cooked, carefully remove the ribs from the smoker and let them rest for 10 minutes before serving. This allows the juices to redistribute, making the meat even more flavorful and tender.
- Slice the ribs between the bones, and serve warm. These smoked beef short ribs with coffee rub are perfect as a hearty main dish and pair beautifully with sides such as coleslaw, roasted vegetables, or mashed potatoes.

HICKORY-SMOKED PORK BELLY WITH ASIAN GLAZE

Prep Time: 20 minutes
Cook Time: 3 hours
Servings: 4
Wood Type: Hickory
Smoking Time: 3 hours

Ingredients

2 lbs pork belly, skin-on
2 tablespoons kosher salt
1 tablespoon freshly ground black pepper
1 tablespoon garlic powder
1 tablespoon onion powder
1/2 cup soy sauce
1/4 cup honey
2 tablespoons rice vinegar
2 tablespoons hoisin sauce
1 tablespoon ginger, grated
2 cloves garlic, minced
1 teaspoon sesame oil
1 teaspoon chili flakes (optional for extra heat)
Sliced green onions, for garnish
Sesame seeds, for garnish

Instructions
- Pat the pork belly dry with paper towels. Mix salt, pepper, garlic powder, and onion powder in a small bowl. Rub this mixture all over the pork belly, ensuring it's fully coated.
- Preheat your electric smoker to 225°F with hickory wood chips ready for smoking.

- Place the pork belly in the smoker, fat side up. Close the smoker and let it cook for about 3 hours, or until the internal temperature reaches 200°F. This low and slow process will render the fat and make the pork belly incredibly tender.
- In a small saucepan, combine soy sauce, honey, rice vinegar, hoisin sauce, grated ginger, minced garlic, sesame oil, and chili flakes (if using). Bring to a simmer over medium heat, stirring occasionally, until the sauce thickens slightly, about 5-7 minutes. Set aside.
- Once the pork belly has reached the desired internal temperature, brush it generously with the Asian glaze. Increase the smoker temperature to 250°F and continue to cook the pork belly for an additional 15-20 minutes, allowing the glaze to caramelize slightly.
- Remove the pork belly from the smoker and let it rest for 10 minutes. Slice it into bite-sized pieces or strips. Drizzle with more glaze if desired, and garnish with sliced green onions and sesame seeds before serving.

SMOKED DUCK BREAST WITH ORANGE BOURBON GLAZE

Prep Time: 20 minutes
Cook Time: 2 hours
Servings: 4
Wood Type: Cherry
Smoking Time: 1.5 to 2 hours

Ingredients
4 duck breasts (about 6 to 8 oz each), skin on
Salt and freshly ground black pepper, to taste
2 tablespoons olive oil
For the Orange Bourbon Glaze:
1 cup freshly squeezed orange juice (about 2-3 oranges)
1/4 cup bourbon
1/4 cup brown sugar
2 tablespoons honey
1 tablespoon soy sauce
1 teaspoon orange zest
1 garlic clove, minced
1/2 teaspoon ground ginger
1/4 teaspoon crushed red pepper flakes (optional for a bit of heat)

Instructions
- Begin by scoring the skin of each duck breast in a diamond pattern, ensuring not to cut into the meat. Season both sides with salt and pepper. Preheat your electric smoker to 225°F with cherry wood chips ready for smoking.
- Place the duck breasts, skin side up, on the smoker rack. Smoke for about 1.5 to 2 hours, or until the internal temperature reaches 135°F for medium-rare. Adjust the smoking time if you prefer your duck more or less done.
- While the duck is smoking, combine the orange juice, bourbon, brown sugar, honey, soy sauce, orange zest, minced garlic, ground ginger, and red pepper flakes (if using) in a small saucepan over medium heat. Bring the mixture to a simmer and reduce it by half or until it thickens enough to coat the back of a spoon, about 10-15 minutes. Remove from heat and set aside.
- Once the duck reaches the desired internal temperature, remove it from the smoker. Heat a skillet over medium-high heat and add olive oil. Sear the duck breasts, skin side down, for 1-2 minutes, or until the skin is crispy. Flip and quickly sear the other side for about 30 seconds.
- Slice the duck breasts thinly. Drizzle with the orange bourbon glaze before serving. You can garnish with additional orange zest or fresh herbs if desired.

CEDAR-SMOKED PRIME RIB WITH GARLIC HERB CRUST

Prep Time: 30 minutes
Cook Time: 2 hours
Servings: 4
Wood Type: Cedar
Smoking Time: 2 hours

Ingredients
1 boneless prime rib roast (about 2-3 lbs)
2 tablespoons olive oil
4 cloves garlic, minced
2 tablespoons fresh rosemary, finely chopped
2 tablespoons fresh thyme, finely chopped
1 tablespoon coarse sea salt
1 teaspoon freshly ground black pepper
1 cedar plank, soaked in water for at least 1 hour

Instructions
- Begin by removing your prime rib from the refrigerator at least 30 minutes before cooking to allow it to come to room temperature. This ensures even cooking.
- While the prime rib is coming to temperature, soak your cedar plank in water for at least 1 hour to prevent it from burning during the smoking process.
- Preheat your electric smoker to 250°F. While it's heating, you can prepare the garlic herb crust.
- In a small bowl, combine the olive oil, minced garlic, rosemary, thyme, coarse sea salt, and black pepper. Mix well to form a paste.
- Rub the garlic herb mixture all over the prime rib, ensuring it is evenly coated on all sides.
- Once the cedar plank is thoroughly soaked, place the prime rib on the plank. This will infuse the meat with a subtle cedar smoke flavor that complements the rich taste of the beef.
- Place the cedar plank with the prime rib in the preheated smoker. Smoke for about 2 hours, or until the internal temperature of the prime rib reaches your desired level of doneness (130°F for medium-rare).
- Once cooked to your liking, remove the prime rib from the smoker and let it rest for at least 20 minutes before slicing. This allows the juices to redistribute throughout the meat, ensuring a moist and flavorful prime rib.
- Slice the prime rib against the grain into thick or thin slices as preferred. Serve immediately, garnished with additional fresh herbs if desired.

SMOKED VENISON LOIN WITH JUNIPER BERRY RUB

Prep Time: 20 minutes
Cook Time: 2 hours
Servings: 4
Wood Type: Apple or Hickory
Smoking Time: 1.5 to 2 hours

Ingredients
2 lbs venison loin, trimmed
2 tbsp juniper berries, crushed
1 tbsp coarse sea salt
1 tbsp cracked black pepper
2 tsp fresh rosemary, finely chopped
2 cloves garlic, minced
1/4 cup olive oil
2 tbsp balsamic vinegar

Instructions
- Begin by patting the venison loin dry with paper towels. This helps the rub adhere better to the meat and ensures a crisp exterior.
- In a small bowl, combine the crushed juniper berries, coarse sea salt, cracked black pepper, finely chopped rosemary, and minced garlic. Mix these ingredients well to create your rub.
- In a separate bowl, whisk together olive oil and balsamic vinegar. Brush this mixture over the venison loin, ensuring it's fully coated.
- Generously apply the juniper berry rub over the loin, pressing gently to adhere it to the surface. Let the venison marinate for at least 30 minutes at room temperature, or for optimal flavor, cover and refrigerate for up to 24 hours.
- Preheat your electric smoker to 225°F, adding apple or hickory wood chips according to the manufacturer's instructions for that smoky flavor.
- Once the smoker is at the right temperature, place the venison loin in the smoker. Smoke the loin for about 1.5 to 2 hours, or until the internal temperature reaches 135°F for medium-rare.
- Remove the venison loin from the smoker and let it rest for 10 minutes. Resting allows the juices to redistribute throughout the meat, ensuring a moist and tender slice.
- Slice the venison loin against the grain into thin slices. Serve immediately, accompanied by your choice of sides, such as roasted vegetables or a fresh salad.

APPLEWOOD-SMOKED CHICKEN THIGHS WITH BBQ SAUCE

Prep Time: 20 minutes
Cook Time: 2 hours
Servings: 4
Wood Type: Applewood
Smoking Time: 1.5 to 2 hours

Ingredients:
8 chicken thighs, bone-in and skin-on
2 tablespoons olive oil
2 teaspoons garlic powder
2 teaspoons smoked paprika
1 teaspoon onion powder
1 teaspoon ground black pepper
1 teaspoon kosher salt
1/2 cup apple cider vinegar
1 cup ketchup
1/4 cup brown sugar
2 tablespoons Worcestershire sauce
1 tablespoon honey
1 teaspoon mustard powder
Applewood chips, for smoking

Instructions:
- Preheat your electric smoker to 225°F. Soak the Applewood chips in water for at least 30 minutes before smoking.
- Pat the chicken thighs dry with paper towels. In a small bowl, mix together the olive oil, garlic powder, smoked paprika, onion powder, ground black pepper, and kosher salt. Rub this mixture all over the chicken thighs, ensuring each piece is well-coated.
- In a medium saucepan over medium heat, combine the apple cider vinegar, ketchup, brown sugar, Worcestershire sauce, honey, and mustard powder. Stir well and bring to a simmer. Let the sauce simmer for about 10 minutes, or until slightly thickened. Adjust seasoning to taste.

- Place the seasoned chicken thighs on the smoker racks. Add the soaked Applewood chips to the smoker. Close the lid and smoke the chicken for about 1.5 to 2 hours, or until the internal temperature reaches 165°F when checked with a meat thermometer.
- During the last 20 minutes of smoking, brush the chicken thighs generously with the BBQ sauce, turning them over once to ensure they are well-coated on all sides.
- Once cooked, remove the chicken thighs from the smoker and let them rest for about 5 minutes. Serve warm with extra BBQ sauce on the side for dipping.
- Your Applewood-Smoked Chicken Thighs with BBQ Sauce are ready to be enjoyed. Pair with your favorite sides such as coleslaw, cornbread, or grilled vegetables for a complete meal.

SMOKED SAUSAGE AND PEPPERS HOAGIES

Prep Time: 15 minutes
Cook Time: 1 hour
Servings: 4
Wood Type: Applewood
Smoking Time: 45 minutes

Ingredients
4 large Italian sausages (about 1 pound)
2 bell peppers (1 red, 1 green), sliced into strips
1 large onion, sliced
2 tablespoons olive oil
Salt and freshly ground black pepper, to taste
4 hoagie rolls, split
1 cup shredded mozzarella cheese (optional)
2 teaspoons of dried oregano
Mustard or mayonnaise, for serving (optional)

Instructions
- Set your electric smoker to 225°F and add applewood chips to the smoker box.
- In a large bowl, toss the sliced bell peppers and onion with olive oil, salt, pepper, and dried oregano until evenly coated.
- Place the Italian sausages and the seasoned vegetables in a single layer on the smoker racks, ensuring they are not overcrowded. Close the smoker lid and smoke for about 45 minutes, or until the sausages are fully cooked (internal temperature of 160°F) and the vegetables are tender and slightly charred.
- During the last 10 minutes of smoking time, open the smoker and place the split hoagie rolls on the top rack to toast lightly. Close the lid and continue smoking.
- Once the sausages and vegetables are done, remove them from the smoker. Slice the sausages if desired. Open the toasted hoagie rolls and evenly distribute the sausage and smoked vegetables among them. If using, sprinkle shredded mozzarella cheese on top of the hot fillings so it melts from the residual heat.
- Optionally, you can add a spread of mustard or mayonnaise to the hoagie rolls before adding the sausage and vegetables. Serve immediately while warm and enjoy the smoky flavors of your homemade Smoked Sausage and Peppers Hoagies.

MESQUITE-SMOKED CATFISH WITH CAJUN SEASONING

Prep Time: 20 minutes
Cook Time: 45 minutes to 1 hour
Servings: 4
Wood Type: Mesquite
Smoking Time: 45 minutes to 1 hour

Ingredients:
4 catfish fillets (about 6-8 ounces each)
2 tablespoons olive oil
For the Cajun Seasoning:
1 tablespoon paprika
1 teaspoon salt
1 teaspoon garlic powder
1 teaspoon onion powder
1 teaspoon ground black pepper
1/2 teaspoon dried thyme
1/2 teaspoon dried oregano
1/2 teaspoon cayenne pepper (adjust based on heat preference)
1/2 teaspoon red pepper flakes (optional for extra heat)

Instructions:
- Rinse the catfish fillets under cold water and pat them dry with paper towels. Ensure they're completely dry to help the seasoning stick and to get a nice, smoky flavor.
- In a small bowl, combine the paprika, salt, garlic powder, onion powder, ground black pepper, dried thyme, dried oregano, cayenne pepper, and red pepper flakes (if using). Mix well to create your Cajun seasoning blend.
- Brush each catfish fillet with olive oil, then rub the Cajun seasoning mix generously over both sides of the fillets. Make sure they are well coated with the seasoning.
- Preheat your electric smoker to 225°F. While it's heating, soak your mesquite wood chips in water for at least 30 minutes.
- Once your smoker is ready, drain the wood chips and add them to the smoker's wood chip compartment. Place the seasoned catfish fillets in the smoker on the racks, ensuring they are not touching for even smoke circulation.
- Close the smoker and let the catfish smoke for about 45 minutes to 1 hour, or until the fish flakes easily with a fork. The internal temperature should reach 145°F when checked with a meat thermometer.
- Remove the catfish from the smoker and let them rest for a few minutes. Serve hot, garnished with lemon wedges and a sprinkle of fresh parsley if desired. This smoky, spicy catfish pairs wonderfully with a side of coleslaw, grilled vegetables, or a fresh garden salad.

CHERRYWOOD-SMOKED MEATLOAF WITH GLAZED TOPPING

Prep Time: 20 minutes
Cook Time: 2 hours 30 minutes
Servings: 4
Wood Type: Cherrywood
Smoking Time: 2 hours 15 minutes

Ingredients
For the Meatloaf:
1 lb ground beef (85% lean)
1 lb ground pork
1 cup breadcrumbs
1 medium onion, finely chopped
2 cloves garlic, minced
1 large egg
1/3 cup milk
2 tablespoons Worcestershire sauce
1 teaspoon salt
1/2 teaspoon ground black pepper

1/2 teaspoon smoked paprika
1/4 cup fresh parsley, chopped
For the Glaze:
1/2 cup ketchup
2 tablespoons brown sugar
1 tablespoon apple cider vinegar
1 teaspoon hot sauce (optional, adjust to taste)
1/2 teaspoon garlic powder

Instructions
- In a large bowl, combine ground beef, ground pork, breadcrumbs, onion, garlic, egg, milk, Worcestershire sauce, salt, pepper, smoked paprika, and parsley. Mix until just combined, being careful not to overmix to keep the meatloaf tender.
- On a baking sheet lined with parchment paper, shape the meat mixture into a loaf approximately 9 inches long and 5 inches wide.
- Preheat your electric smoker to 225°F with cherrywood chips ready for smoking.
- Place the meatloaf (on the baking sheet) in the smoker. Close the lid and smoke for about 2 hours 15 minutes, or until the internal temperature reaches 160°F.
- While the meatloaf is smoking, mix ketchup, brown sugar, apple cider vinegar, hot sauce, and garlic powder in a small bowl. Set aside for later.
- In the last 15 minutes of smoking, brush the meatloaf generously with the glaze. Continue to smoke for the remaining time to allow the glaze to caramelize slightly.
- Once done, remove the meatloaf from the smoker and let it rest for 10 minutes before slicing. This allows the juices to redistribute, ensuring the meatloaf is moist and flavorful.
- Slice the meatloaf and serve with sides of your choice, such as mashed potatoes, steamed green beans, or a simple salad for a complete meal.

SMOKED BISON BURGERS WITH BLUE CHEESE

Prep Time: 20 minutes
Cook Time: 1 hour
Servings: 4
Wood Type: Hickory
Smoking Time: 45 minutes to 1 hour

Ingredients:
1 pound ground bison meat
1/2 cup crumbled blue cheese
1/4 cup minced red onion
1 clove garlic, minced
2 tablespoons Worcestershire sauce
1 teaspoon salt
1/2 teaspoon ground black pepper
4 hamburger buns
Optional toppings: lettuce, tomato slices, red onion rings

Instructions:
- In a large bowl, combine the ground bison, crumbled blue cheese, minced red onion, minced garlic, Worcestershire sauce, salt, and pepper. Be careful not to overmix to keep the burgers juicy.
- Divide the mixture into 4 equal portions. Form each portion into a patty about 1/2 inch thick. Make a slight indentation in the center of each patty to prevent bulging during cooking.
- Preheat your electric smoker to 225°F using hickory wood chips. The hickory wood will impart a rich, slightly sweet smoke flavor that complements the bison and blue cheese beautifully.

- Place the patties on the smoker's grill grate. Close the lid and smoke for about 45 minutes to 1 hour, or until the internal temperature of the burgers reaches 145°F for medium-rare or 160°F for medium. Use a meat thermometer to ensure accurate cooking.
- Once done, transfer the burgers to a plate and let them rest for a few minutes. Resting allows the juices to redistribute throughout the burger, making it moist and flavorful.
- During the last few minutes of cooking, you can optionally add the hamburger buns to the smoker to warm and lightly toast them.
- Place each smoked bison burger on a bun bottom. Add your choice of optional toppings like lettuce, tomato slices, and onion rings. Cap with the bun tops.
- Serve the smoked bison burgers immediately, allowing each person to add additional toppings and condiments as they prefer.

HICKORY-SMOKED PORK LOIN WITH APPLE CIDER GLAZE

Prep Time: 30 minutes
Cook Time: 2 hours
Servings: 4
Wood Type: Hickory
Smoking Time: 1.5 to 2 hours

Ingredients:
2 lb pork loin
2 tablespoons olive oil
2 teaspoons salt
1 teaspoon freshly ground black pepper
1 teaspoon garlic powder
1 teaspoon onion powder
1 teaspoon smoked paprika
1/2 cup apple cider
1/4 cup apple cider vinegar
1/4 cup brown sugar
1 tablespoon Dijon mustard
1 teaspoon Worcestershire sauce
Hickory wood chips, for smoking

Instructions:
- Rinse the pork loin under cold water and pat dry with paper towels. In a small bowl, mix together the salt, black pepper, garlic powder, onion powder, and smoked paprika. Rub the olive oil over the entire surface of the pork loin, then evenly coat it with the spice mixture.
- Preheat your electric smoker to 225°F with hickory wood chips ready for use.
- Once the smoker is at the desired temperature, place the pork loin in the smoker. Smoke the pork loin for about 1.5 to 2 hours, or until the internal temperature reaches 145°F. Use a meat thermometer to ensure accuracy.
- While the pork is smoking, combine the apple cider, apple cider vinegar, brown sugar, Dijon mustard, and Worcestershire sauce in a small saucepan over medium heat. Reduce the heat to low and let it simmer for 10-15 minutes, or until the glaze has thickened slightly. Remove from heat and set aside.
- In the last 15-20 minutes of smoking, brush the pork loin with the apple cider glaze. Continue to smoke until the glazing is done.
- Once the pork loin is cooked, remove it from the smoker and let it rest for 10 minutes. Slice the pork loin and serve it with additional apple cider glaze drizzled over the top.

ALDER-SMOKED QUAIL WITH WILD RICE STUFFING

Prep Time: 30 minutes
Cook Time: 1 hour
Servings: 4
Wood Type: Alder
Smoking Time: 45 minutes to 1 hour

Ingredients
For the Quail:
4 whole quails, cleaned and ready for stuffing
2 tablespoons olive oil
1 teaspoon salt
1/2 teaspoon black pepper
1/2 teaspoon garlic powder
1/2 teaspoon dried thyme
For the Wild Rice Stuffing:
1 cup wild rice, rinsed
2 cups chicken broth
1 bay leaf
1 tablespoon olive oil
1/2 cup diced onions
1/2 cup diced celery
1/2 cup diced carrots
2 cloves garlic, minced
1/4 cup dried cranberries
1/4 cup chopped pecans
1 teaspoon salt
1/2 teaspoon black pepper

Instructions
- In a medium saucepan, combine the wild rice, chicken broth, and bay leaf. Bring to a boil, then reduce heat to low, cover, and simmer for 45-50 minutes, or until the rice is tender and the liquid is absorbed.
- In a skillet over medium heat, heat the olive oil. Add the onions, celery, and carrots. Sauté until the vegetables are soft, about 5 minutes. Add the garlic and sauté for another minute.
- Once the rice is cooked, remove the bay leaf and mix the rice with the sautéed vegetables, dried cranberries, chopped pecans, salt, and pepper. Set aside to cool slightly before stuffing the quail.
- Preheat your electric smoker to 225°F and add alder wood chips according to the manufacturer's instructions.
- Rinse the quails and pat them dry. Lightly season the inside and outside of each quail with salt, pepper, garlic powder, and dried thyme.
- Stuff each quail with the wild rice stuffing, then truss the legs together with kitchen twine to help hold the stuffing inside during cooking.
- Place the stuffed quails on the smoker rack. Close the smoker and smoke the quail for 45 minutes to 1 hour, or until the internal temperature of the stuffing reaches 165°F and the quails are golden and slightly crispy.
- Halfway through the smoking process, brush the quails with olive oil to help crisp the skin.
- Remove the quails from the smoker and let them rest for 10 minutes before serving. This allows the juices to redistribute throughout the meat, ensuring a moist and flavorful bite.
- Serve the alder-smoked quail with additional sides if desired, such as a simple green salad or roasted vegetables.

PECAN-SMOKED LEG OF LAMB WITH MINT PESTO

Prep Time: 30 minutes
Cook Time: 2.5 hours
Servings: 4
Wood Type: Pecan
Smoking Time: 2 hours

Ingredients
For the Lamb:
2 to 3 lb leg of lamb, boneless and trimmed
2 tablespoons olive oil
4 garlic cloves, minced
1 tablespoon fresh rosemary, finely chopped
1 teaspoon salt
1/2 teaspoon freshly ground black pepper
For the Mint Pesto:
1 cup fresh mint leaves
1/2 cup fresh parsley leaves
1/4 cup parmesan cheese, grated
1/4 cup pine nuts or walnuts
2 garlic cloves
1/2 cup olive oil
Salt and pepper, to taste

Instructions
- In a small bowl, mix together olive oil, minced garlic, rosemary, salt, and pepper. Rub this mixture all over the lamb leg, ensuring it's fully coated.
- Let the lamb marinate for at least 30 minutes in the refrigerator, or for best results, overnight.
- Preheat your electric smoker to 225°F with pecan wood chips ready for smoking.
- Once the smoker is preheated, place the lamb leg in the smoker.
- Smoke the lamb for about 2 hours, or until the internal temperature reaches 145°F for medium-rare, or 160°F for medium.
- Once cooked to your liking, remove the lamb from the smoker and let it rest for 10-15 minutes. This allows the juices to redistribute, making the meat more tender and flavorful.
- In a food processor, combine mint leaves, parsley, parmesan cheese, nuts, and garlic cloves. Pulse until coarsely chopped.
- With the processor running, gradually add olive oil until the pesto reaches your desired consistency. Season with salt and pepper to taste.
- Slice the smoked lamb leg thinly against the grain.
- Serve the slices drizzled with the fresh mint pesto.

CEDAR-PLANK SMOKED SALMON WITH DILL SAUCE

Prep Time: 20 minutes
Cook Time: 20 minutes
Servings: 4
Wood Type: Cedar
Smoking Time: 1 hour

Ingredients:
1 large cedar plank (at least 12 inches in length, pre-soaked in water for 2 hours)
4 salmon fillets (6 ounces each, skin on)
2 tablespoons olive oil

Salt and freshly ground black pepper, to taste
1 lemon, thinly sliced (for garnish)
For the Dill Sauce:
1 cup sour cream
2 tablespoons fresh dill, chopped
1 tablespoon lemon juice
1 teaspoon lemon zest
1 small garlic clove, minced
Salt and freshly ground black pepper, to taste

Instructions:
- Preheat your electric smoker to 225°F and place the soaked cedar plank inside to warm up. This helps in imparting a gentle cedar aroma to the salmon.
- While the smoker preheats, prepare the salmon fillets. Brush each fillet lightly with olive oil, then season both sides with salt and pepper.
- Once the smoker reaches the desired temperature and the cedar plank is warm, place the salmon fillets on the plank, skin-side down. Close the smoker lid and smoke the salmon for about 1 hour, or until the salmon is cooked through and flakes easily with a fork.
- While the salmon is smoking, prepare the dill sauce. In a small bowl, mix together sour cream, chopped dill, lemon juice, lemon zest, minced garlic, salt, and pepper. Adjust the seasoning to taste and set aside in the refrigerator to chill.
- Once the salmon is done, carefully remove the cedar plank from the smoker using heat-resistant gloves.
- Plate each salmon fillet, and generously drizzle with the chilled dill sauce. Garnish with additional lemon slices and fresh dill, if desired. Serve immediately for the best taste.

SMOKED BRISKET CHILI

Prep Time: 20 minutes
Cook Time: 3 hours
Servings: 4
Wood Type: Mesquite
Smoking Time: 2 hours

Ingredients
1 lb smoked brisket, cubed
1 large onion, diced
3 cloves garlic, minced
1 green bell pepper, diced
1 can (14.5 oz) diced tomatoes
1 can (15 oz) kidney beans, drained and rinsed
1 can (15 oz) black beans, drained and rinsed
2 tablespoons tomato paste
2 cups beef broth
2 tablespoons chili powder
1 teaspoon ground cumin
1 teaspoon smoked paprika
1/2 teaspoon ground coriander
Salt and pepper to taste
Olive oil
Optional for garnish: shredded cheddar cheese, sour cream, chopped green onions, cilantro

Instructions
- Begin by smoking your brisket with mesquite wood at 225°F for about 2 hours or until it reaches an internal temperature of 195°F. Once smoked, let it rest before cubing it into bite-sized pieces.

- In a large pot over medium heat, add a splash of olive oil. Add the diced onion, minced garlic, and green bell pepper. Cook until the vegetables are soft and the onions are translucent, about 5-7 minutes.
- Add the cubed smoked brisket to the pot along with the diced tomatoes, kidney beans, black beans, tomato paste, beef broth, chili powder, ground cumin, smoked paprika, and ground coriander. Stir well to combine all the ingredients.
- Bring the chili to a simmer and then reduce the heat to low. Cover and let it cook for about 3 hours, stirring occasionally.
- After simmering, taste the chili and season with salt and pepper as needed.
- Serve the chili in bowls, garnished with shredded cheddar cheese, sour cream, chopped green onions, and cilantro if desired.

APPLEWOOD-SMOKED TURKEY LEGS WITH HONEY MUSTARD

Prep Time: 30 minutes
Cook Time: 4 hours
Servings: 4
Wood Type: Applewood
Smoking Time: 4 hours

Ingredients:
4 large turkey legs, skin on
2 tablespoons olive oil
1 tablespoon sea salt
2 teaspoons freshly ground black pepper
2 teaspoons garlic powder
2 teaspoons onion powder
2 teaspoons smoked paprika
1 cup apple cider
For the Honey Mustard Glaze:
1/2 cup Dijon mustard
1/4 cup honey
1 tablespoon apple cider vinegar
1 teaspoon garlic powder
Salt and pepper to taste

Instructions:
- Rinse the turkey legs under cold water and pat them dry with paper towels. Ensure they are completely dry to help the smoke adhere better.
- In a small bowl, combine the olive oil, sea salt, black pepper, garlic powder, onion powder, and smoked paprika. Rub this mixture all over the turkey legs, making sure they are well-coated.
- Preheat your electric smoker to 225°F and add the applewood chips to the smoker's wood chip compartment. Wait until the smoker is producing a steady stream of smoke.
- Place the turkey legs in the smoker, making sure they are not touching each other to allow the smoke to circulate freely.
- Smoke the turkey legs for about 4 hours, or until the internal temperature reaches 165°F. Halfway through the smoking process, baste the turkey legs with apple cider to keep them moist and flavorful.
- While the turkey legs are smoking, prepare the honey mustard glaze. In a small bowl, whisk together the Dijon mustard, honey, apple cider vinegar, garlic powder, salt, and pepper until smooth.
- In the last 30 minutes of smoking, generously brush the honey mustard glaze over the turkey legs. Continue to smoke for the remaining time to allow the glaze to caramelize slightly.
- Once done, remove the turkey legs from the smoker and let them rest for about 10 minutes before serving. This allows the juices to redistribute, making the meat even more succulent.

SMOKED PASTRAMI ON RYE WITH MUSTARD

Prep Time: 20 minutes
Cook Time: 3 hours
Servings: 4
Wood Type: Hickory or Applewood
Smoking Time: 3 hours

Ingredients:
For the Pastrami:
2 lbs beef brisket, trimmed
2 tablespoons coriander seeds
2 tablespoons black peppercorns
1 tablespoon mustard seeds
1 tablespoon brown sugar
2 teaspoons garlic powder
2 teaspoons onion powder
1 teaspoon paprika
1/2 teaspoon cayenne pepper (optional, for a bit of heat)
Salt to taste
For Serving:
8 slices of rye bread
Mustard, preferably whole grain or Dijon
Pickles, for serving on the side

Instructions:
- In a small bowl, combine the coriander seeds, black peppercorns, and mustard seeds. Using a spice grinder or a mortar and pestle, coarsely grind the spices.
- Mix the ground spices with brown sugar, garlic powder, onion powder, paprika, and cayenne pepper in a bowl to create your pastrami rub.
- Generously season the beef brisket on all sides with salt, then coat evenly with the spice rub. Let it sit at room temperature for about 1 hour or refrigerate overnight for deeper flavor penetration.
- Soak your wood chips in water for at least 30 minutes before smoking. Preheat your electric smoker to 250°F, using hickory or applewood chips for the smoke.
- Place the brisket in the smoker and smoke for about 3 hours, or until the internal temperature reaches 190°F. Ensure to maintain a consistent smoke throughout the cooking time.
- Once done, remove the pastrami from the smoker and wrap it in aluminum foil. Let it rest for about 20 minutes. This allows the juices to redistribute throughout the meat, ensuring it's moist and flavorful.
- Slice the pastrami against the grain into thin slices. Serve on rye bread with a generous spread of mustard and pickles on the side.

HICKORY-SMOKED HAM WITH PINEAPPLE BROWN SUGAR GLAZE

Prep Time: 20 minutes
Cook Time: 3 hours
Servings: 4
Wood Type: Hickory
Smoking Time: 3 hours

Ingredients:
2-3 lb boneless ham, fully cooked
1 cup pineapple juice
1 cup brown sugar
2 tablespoons Dijon mustard

1 tablespoon apple cider vinegar
1/2 teaspoon ground cloves
1/2 teaspoon garlic powder
Hickory wood chips, soaked in water for at least 30 minutes

Instructions:
- Preheat your electric smoker to 250°F and add the soaked hickory wood chips to the smoker's wood chip box.
- In a medium saucepan over medium heat, combine the pineapple juice, brown sugar, Dijon mustard, apple cider vinegar, ground cloves, and garlic powder. Stir until the brown sugar has dissolved and the mixture begins to slightly thicken, about 5-7 minutes. Remove from heat and let the glaze cool slightly.
- Place the ham in the smoker on the middle rack. Using a basting brush, generously apply a layer of the pineapple brown sugar glaze over the entire surface of the ham.
- Close the smoker lid and smoke the ham for about 3 hours, or until the internal temperature of the ham reaches 140°F. Baste the ham with the glaze every 45 minutes to ensure it stays moist and flavorful.
- Once the ham is fully cooked, remove it from the smoker and let it rest for 10 minutes before slicing. This allows the juices to redistribute throughout the meat, ensuring it's moist and flavorful.
- Serve the hickory-smoked ham slices with any remaining glaze drizzled on top or on the side as a dipping sauce.

CEDAR-PLANKED SMOKED SALMON WITH LEMON DILL SAUCE

Prep Time: 15 minutes
Cook Time: 25 minutes
Servings: 4
Wood Type: Cedar
Smoking Time: 20 to 25 minutes

Ingredients:
For the Salmon:
1 large cedar plank (soaked in water for at least 2 hours)
4 salmon fillets (about 6 ounces each)
Salt and freshly ground black pepper, to taste
2 tablespoons olive oil
1 lemon, thinly sliced (for garnish)
For the Lemon Dill Sauce:
1 cup sour cream
2 tablespoons fresh dill, chopped
1 tablespoon lemon juice
1 teaspoon lemon zest
1 clove garlic, minced
Salt and freshly ground black pepper, to taste

Instructions:
- Preheat your electric smoker to 225°F with the lid closed. Ensure the cedar plank is fully submerged in water for at least 2 hours before use to avoid burning.
- While the smoker preheats, prepare your salmon fillets. Rinse them under cold water and pat dry with paper towels. Season both sides of the salmon with salt and pepper, then brush them lightly with olive oil.
- Remove the cedar plank from the water and place it in the smoker for about 3 minutes, or until it starts to crackle and smoke slightly. Carefully remove the plank using tongs, and place the salmon fillets on top of the plank.
- Transfer the cedar plank with the salmon into the preheated smoker. Close the lid and smoke for 20 to 25 minutes, or until the salmon is opaque and flakes easily with a fork.
- While the salmon is smoking, prepare the sauce. In a small bowl, combine sour cream, chopped dill, lemon juice, lemon zest, and minced garlic. Season with salt and pepper to taste. Stir until well combined and set aside in the refrigerator until ready to serve.
- Once the salmon is done, carefully remove the cedar plank from the smoker and transfer the salmon fillets to a serving platter. Garnish with lemon slices and serve immediately with the lemon dill sauce on the side.

HICKORY-SMOKED SHRIMP SKEWERS WITH GARLIC BUTTER

Prep Time: 15 minutes
Cook Time: 10 minutes
Servings: 4
Wood Type: Hickory
Smoking Time: 30 minutes to 1 hour for pre-smoking the wood chips (if your smoker requires pre-smoking)

Ingredients
1 pound large shrimp, peeled and deveined (tail on)
2 tablespoons olive oil
1 teaspoon paprika
1 teaspoon garlic powder
1/2 teaspoon salt
1/4 teaspoon black pepper
1/4 teaspoon red pepper flakes (optional for a spicy kick)
2 tablespoons unsalted butter
2 garlic cloves, minced
Juice of 1 lemon
Fresh parsley, chopped (for garnish)
Wooden skewers, soaked in water for at least 30 minutes

Instructions
- Start by soaking your wooden skewers in water for at least 30 minutes to prevent them from burning. Preheat your electric smoker to 225°F with hickory wood chips ready for smoking.
- In a large bowl, combine olive oil, paprika, garlic powder, salt, black pepper, and red pepper flakes. Add the shrimp and toss until they are evenly coated. Let them marinate for about 10-15 minutes.
- Thread the marinated shrimp onto the soaked skewers, leaving a small space between each shrimp to ensure even smoking.
- While the shrimp marinate, melt the butter in a small saucepan over medium heat. Add the minced garlic and cook until it's fragrant but not browned. Remove from heat and stir in the lemon juice. Set aside.
- Place the shrimp skewers in the smoker. Smoke for about 30 minutes to 1 hour, or until the shrimp are pink and slightly opaque. The exact time will depend on your smoker and the size of the shrimp.
- Once the shrimp are done, carefully remove them from the smoker. Brush the shrimp generously with the garlic butter mixture and garnish with chopped parsley.
- Serve the hickory-smoked shrimp skewers immediately, with extra lemon wedges on the side for those who love a zesty kick.

ALDER-SMOKED SCALLOPS WITH BACON JAM

Prep Time: 20 minutes
Cook Time: 1 hour
Servings: 4
Wood Type: Alder
Smoking Time: 20 minutes

Ingredients
For the Scallops:
12 large sea scallops, muscle removed
2 tablespoons olive oil
Salt and freshly ground black pepper, to taste
1 teaspoon smoked paprika
For the Bacon Jam:
1/2 pound thick-cut bacon, cut into 1-inch pieces
1 large onion, finely chopped
2 cloves garlic, minced
1/4 cup apple cider vinegar
1/4 cup brown sugar
1/4 cup pure maple syrup
1/2 cup brewed coffee
Salt and freshly ground black pepper, to taste

Instructions
- In a medium skillet over medium heat, cook the bacon until it begins to crisp. Remove bacon and set aside, leaving about 2 tablespoons of bacon fat in the skillet.
- Add the onion and garlic to the skillet and cook until the onion is translucent, about 5 minutes.
- Return the bacon to the skillet, adding the apple cider vinegar, brown sugar, maple syrup, and coffee. Simmer the mixture on low heat, stirring occasionally, until it thickens and becomes jam-like, about 30 minutes. Season with salt and pepper to taste. Set aside to cool.
- Preheat your electric smoker to 225°F and add alder wood chips to the smoker's wood chip tray.
- Pat the scallops dry with paper towels. In a bowl, toss scallops with olive oil, smoked paprika, salt, and pepper until evenly coated.
- Place scallops on a grill mat or smoker rack, ensuring they are not touching for even smoke circulation.
- Smoke the scallops for about 20 minutes, or until they are opaque and slightly firm to the touch.
- Spoon a generous amount of bacon jam onto each plate.
- Place three smoked scallops on top of the bacon jam on each plate.
- Optionally, garnish with fresh herbs or a drizzle of olive oil before serving.

MESQUITE-SMOKED CRAB CAKES WITH REMOULADE

Prep Time: 30 minutes
Cook Time: 10 minutes
Servings: 4
Wood Type: Mesquite
Smoking Time: 20 minutes

Ingredients
For the Crab Cakes:
1 pound lump crab meat, carefully picked over for shells
1/4 cup mayonnaise
1 large egg, lightly beaten
1 tablespoon Dijon mustard
1 teaspoon Worcestershire sauce
1/2 teaspoon hot sauce (adjust to taste)
1/4 cup finely chopped green onions
1/4 cup finely chopped parsley
1 cup panko breadcrumbs, divided
Salt and freshly ground black pepper, to taste
Olive oil or non-stick cooking spray (for the smoker rack)
For the Remoulade:
1/2 cup mayonnaise
1 tablespoon capers, chopped
1 tablespoon Dijon mustard
1 tablespoon prepared horseradish
1 tablespoon finely chopped parsley
1 teaspoon paprika
1 clove garlic, minced
2 tablespoons lemon juice
Salt and freshly ground black pepper, to taste

Instructions
- In a large bowl, combine the lump crab meat, 1/4 cup mayonnaise, beaten egg, Dijon mustard, Worcestershire sauce, hot sauce, green onions, parsley, and 1/2 cup of the panko breadcrumbs. Season with salt and pepper to taste. Gently fold the ingredients together until just combined, being careful not to break up the crab meat too much.

- Divide the crab mixture into 8 equal portions and shape each into a patty. Coat each patty with the remaining panko breadcrumbs, pressing gently to adhere. Place the crab cakes on a plate, cover, and refrigerate for at least 15 minutes to set.
- Preheat your electric smoker to 225°F and add mesquite wood chips according to the manufacturer's instructions for a medium smoke flavor.
- Lightly oil the smoker rack or use non-stick cooking spray to prevent sticking. Place the crab cakes on the rack, leaving some space between each for the smoke to circulate. Close the smoker and smoke the crab cakes for 20 minutes, or until they are firm and cooked through.
- While the crab cakes are smoking, prepare the remoulade by combining 1/2 cup mayonnaise, chopped capers, Dijon mustard, horseradish, chopped parsley, paprika, minced garlic, and lemon juice in a small bowl. Season with salt and pepper to taste, and mix well. Refrigerate until ready to serve.
- Once the crab cakes are done smoking, carefully remove them from the smoker. Serve immediately with a generous dollop of the remoulade sauce on the side or drizzled on top.

CHERRYWOOD-SMOKED LOBSTER TAILS WITH HERB BUTTER

Prep Time: 20 minutes
Cook Time: 45 minutes to 1 hour
Servings: 4
Wood Type: Cherrywood
Smoking Time: 45 minutes to 1 hour

Ingredients
4 lobster tails (4 to 5 ounces each)
1 cup unsalted butter, softened
2 tablespoons fresh parsley, finely chopped
1 tablespoon fresh chives, finely chopped
2 cloves garlic, minced
1 teaspoon lemon zest
2 teaspoons lemon juice
Salt and pepper, to taste
Cherrywood chips, for smoking

Instructions
- Preheat your electric smoker to 225°F. Soak cherrywood chips in water for at least 30 minutes prior to smoking.
- Using sharp kitchen shears, cut down the middle of the lobster tail shells, stopping at the tail fin.
- In a small bowl, combine softened butter, parsley, chives, garlic, lemon zest, and lemon juice. Season with salt and pepper to taste. Mix well until all ingredients are thoroughly incorporated.
- Generously brush the lobster meat with the herb butter mixture. Reserve some butter for serving.
- Place the lobster tails in the smoker, meat side up. Add the soaked cherrywood chips to the smoker. Smoke the lobster tails for 45 minutes to 1 hour, or until the meat is opaque and cooked through. The internal temperature should reach 140°F when checked with a meat thermometer.
- Remove the lobster tails from the smoker. Let them rest for a few minutes before serving. Serve with additional herb butter on the side for dipping.

SMOKED OYSTERS WITH SPICY MIGNONETTE

Prep Time: 20 minutes
Cook Time: 10 minutes
Servings: 4
Wood Type: Apple or Cherry
Smoking Time: 10 minutes

Ingredients:
For the Oysters:
24 fresh oysters, in the shell
2 cups rock salt or ice, for serving
For the Spicy Mignonette:
1/2 cup red wine vinegar
1 tablespoon shallots, finely minced
1 teaspoon black peppercorns, freshly cracked
1/2 teaspoon red pepper flakes (adjust to taste)
1 teaspoon honey (optional, for balance)
Salt, to taste
2 tablespoons fresh parsley, finely chopped (for garnish)

Instructions:
- Preheat your electric smoker to 225°F, using apple or cherry wood chips for a subtly sweet and smoky flavor.
- Rinse the oysters under cold water, scrubbing any dirt or debris off their shells. Shuck the oysters, being careful to keep them on the half shell. Discard the top shells.
- In a small bowl, combine the red wine vinegar, minced shallots, cracked black peppercorns, red pepper flakes, and honey if using. Mix well until the honey is dissolved and ingredients are well combined. Season with salt to taste. Set aside to let the flavors meld.
- Place the shucked oysters on a bed of rock salt or ice in a tray. This helps keep them stable and level in the smoker.
- Carefully transfer the tray into the preheated smoker. Smoke the oysters for about 10 minutes, or until they are just heated through and slightly firmer.
- Remove the oysters from the smoker and arrange them on a serving platter filled with rock salt or crushed ice to keep them in place.
- Spoon a small amount of the spicy mignonette over each oyster.
- Garnish with freshly chopped parsley.
- Serve immediately, allowing guests to enjoy the warmth of the smoked oysters contrasted with the sharp, spicy kick of the mignonette.

APPLEWOOD-SMOKED TROUT WITH ALMOND CRUST

Prep Time: 20 minutes
Cook Time: 1 hour 30 minutes
Servings: 4
Wood Type: Applewood
Smoking Time: 1 hour to 1 hour 15 minutes

Ingredients:
4 whole trout, cleaned and gutted
2 tablespoons olive oil
1 teaspoon sea salt
1/2 teaspoon freshly ground black pepper
1/4 cup finely chopped almonds
2 tablespoons fresh dill, chopped
2 teaspoons lemon zest
4 lemon slices, for serving
Additional dill sprigs, for garnish

Instructions:

- Preheat your electric smoker to 225°F and add applewood chips to the smoker box. Ensure the trout are fully thawed if previously frozen, rinsed, and patted dry with paper towels.
- Lightly brush the trout inside and out with olive oil. Season the inside with salt and pepper. In a small bowl, mix the chopped almonds, dill, and lemon zest. Divide the almond mixture evenly and stuff it into the cavity of each trout.
- Place the trout directly on the smoker racks or in a fish basket if preferred. Close the smoker lid and smoke the trout for 1 hour to 1 hour 15 minutes, or until the fish flakes easily with a fork and reaches an internal temperature of 145°F.
- Carefully remove the trout from the smoker and let them rest for a few minutes. Serve each trout with a slice of lemon and garnish with fresh dill sprigs. Offer additional salt and pepper to taste.

SMOKED MUSSELS WITH TOMATO AND CHORIZO

Prep Time: 20 minutes
Cook Time: 40 minutes
Servings: 4
Wood Type: Apple or Cherry
Smoking Time: 20 minutes

Ingredients:
2 pounds fresh mussels, cleaned and debearded
1/2 pound chorizo, diced
1 medium onion, finely chopped
3 cloves garlic, minced
1 can (14 ounces) diced tomatoes, drained
1/2 cup white wine
1/4 cup fresh parsley, chopped
2 tablespoons olive oil
1 teaspoon smoked paprika
Salt and pepper to taste
Crusty bread, for serving

Instructions:
- Start by cleaning the mussels under cold running water. Scrub the shells and remove the beards (the stringy bits hanging from the mussel shells). Discard any mussels that are open and do not close when tapped.
- Dice the chorizo into small pieces, chop the onion and garlic finely, and drain the canned tomatoes.
- Preheat your electric smoker to 225°F using apple or cherry wood chips for a sweet and mild smoke flavor.
- In a large pan over medium heat, add the olive oil and chorizo. Cook for about 5 minutes, or until the chorizo starts to release its oils.
- Add the onion and garlic to the pan with chorizo, cooking until they are soft and fragrant, about 5 minutes.
- Stir in the smoked paprika, diced tomatoes, and white wine. Bring the mixture to a simmer and cook for 10 minutes, allowing the flavors to meld together. Season with salt and pepper to taste.
- Transfer the tomato and chorizo mixture to a disposable aluminum pan that can fit in your smoker.
- Nestle the cleaned mussels into the mixture, ensuring they are partly submerged.
- Place the pan in the preheated smoker. Smoke the mussels for about 20 minutes, or until they open up. Discard any mussels that do not open.
- Once the mussels are cooked, sprinkle chopped parsley over the top for a fresh burst of flavor.
- Taste and adjust seasoning if necessary.
- Serve the smoked mussels with tomato and chorizo hot, accompanied by crusty bread to soak up the delicious sauce.

HICKORY-SMOKED CATFISH PO'BOYS

Prep Time: 20 minutes
Cook Time: 45 minutes
Servings: 4
Wood Type: Hickory
Smoking Time: 30-35 minutes

Ingredients:
4 catfish fillets, about 6 ounces each
1 tablespoon olive oil
1 tablespoon Cajun seasoning
2 teaspoons garlic powder
1 teaspoon smoked paprika
Salt and black pepper to taste
1 cup all-purpose flour
4 French rolls or hoagie buns, split and lightly toasted
1/2 cup mayonnaise
1 tablespoon hot sauce (adjust to taste)
2 cups shredded lettuce
1 large tomato, thinly sliced
Dill pickle slices, for garnish
Lemon wedges, for serving

Instructions:
- Rinse the catfish fillets under cold water and pat dry with paper towels. In a small bowl, combine the olive oil, Cajun seasoning, garlic powder, smoked paprika, salt, and black pepper. Rub this mixture evenly over both sides of the catfish fillets.
- Preheat your electric smoker to 225°F with hickory wood chips ready for smoking.
- Place the all-purpose flour in a shallow dish. Lightly dredge the seasoned catfish fillets in the flour, shaking off any excess.
- Once the smoker is at the right temperature, place the catfish fillets on the smoker rack. Close the lid and smoke for 30-35 minutes, or until the catfish is flaky and reaches an internal temperature of 145°F.
- While the catfish is smoking, mix together the mayonnaise and hot sauce in a small bowl. Adjust the hot sauce to suit your taste.
- Spread the spicy mayonnaise on the cut sides of the toasted French rolls. On the bottom half of each roll, layer the shredded lettuce, followed by slices of smoked catfish. Top with tomato slices and pickle slices. Cover with the top half of the roll.
- Cut each Po'Boy in half and serve immediately with lemon wedges on the side for a zesty kick.

CEDAR-SMOKED SALMON NICOISE SALAD

Prep Time: 20 minutes
Cook Time: 1 hour (including rest time for the salmon)
Servings: 4
Wood Type: Cedar
Smoking Time: 45 minutes

Ingredients:
For the Cedar-Smoked Salmon:
4 (6-ounce) salmon fillets, skin on
2 tablespoons olive oil
1 tablespoon sea salt
1 teaspoon freshly ground black pepper

1 cedar plank, soaked in water for at least 1 hour
For the Salad:
8 cups mixed salad greens (such as arugula, spinach, and romaine)
1 pound small new potatoes, boiled until tender and halved
4 hard-boiled eggs, quartered
1 cup cherry tomatoes, halved
1/2 cup pitted Kalamata olives
1/2 cup thinly sliced red onion
1/4 cup capers, rinsed
For the Dressing:
1/3 cup extra-virgin olive oil
2 tablespoons red wine vinegar
1 tablespoon Dijon mustard
1 garlic clove, minced
Salt and pepper to taste
Instructions:

- Preheat your electric smoker to 225°F and place the soaked cedar plank inside.
- Rub each salmon fillet with olive oil, and season with sea salt and black pepper.
- Once the smoker is ready, place the salmon fillets on the cedar plank.
- Smoke for 45 minutes, or until the salmon reaches an internal temperature of 145°F.
- Remove the salmon from the smoker and let it rest for at least 10 minutes before flaking into large pieces with a fork.
- In a large bowl, combine the mixed salad greens, boiled new potatoes, hard-boiled eggs, cherry tomatoes, Kalamata olives, red onion, and capers.
- In a small bowl, whisk together the extra-virgin olive oil, red wine vinegar, Dijon mustard, minced garlic, salt, and pepper to create the dressing.
- Drizzle the dressing over the salad and gently toss to combine.
- Divide the salad among four plates.
- Top each salad with an equal amount of flaked cedar-smoked salmon.
- Serve immediately, offering additional dressing on the side if desired.

MESQUITE-SMOKED TILAPIA TACOS WITH SLAW

Prep Time: 20 minutes
Cook Time: 30-40 minutes
Servings: 4
Wood Type: Mesquite
Smoking Time: 20-30 minutes

Ingredients
For the Tilapia:
4 tilapia fillets (about 6 ounces each)
2 tablespoons olive oil
1 teaspoon smoked paprika
1 teaspoon garlic powder
Salt and pepper to taste
1 lime, juiced
For the Slaw:
2 cups shredded red cabbage
1 cup shredded carrot
1/2 cup thinly sliced red onion
1/4 cup chopped fresh cilantro
2 tablespoons mayonnaise
1 tablespoon apple cider vinegar
Salt and pepper to taste

1 lime, juiced
Additional:
8 small corn tortillas
Mesquite wood chips, for smoking
Optional garnishes: sliced avocado, lime wedges, sour cream, hot sauce

Instructions
- In a small bowl, combine olive oil, smoked paprika, garlic powder, salt, pepper, and lime juice. Rub this mixture all over the tilapia fillets. Let them marinate for 15 minutes.
- Preheat your electric smoker to 225°F and add mesquite wood chips according to the manufacturer's instructions.
- Place the tilapia fillets in the smoker. Smoke for 20-30 minutes, or until the fish is opaque and flakes easily with a fork.
- While the fish is smoking, in a large bowl, combine red cabbage, carrot, red onion, cilantro, mayonnaise, apple cider vinegar, salt, pepper, and lime juice. Toss well to combine and set aside.
- Wrap the tortillas in foil and warm them in the smoker during the last 5 minutes of cooking time, or heat them in a dry skillet over medium heat for about 30 seconds on each side.
- Flake the smoked tilapia with a fork. On each tortilla, layer a generous amount of slaw and tilapia. Garnish with avocado slices, lime wedges, sour cream, and hot sauce if desired.
- Serve immediately, accompanied by the remaining lime wedges on the side for an extra squirt of lime juice if desired.

SMOKED SHRIMP AND GRITS

Prep Time: 20 minutes
Cook Time: 1 hour
Servings: 4
Wood Type: Apple or Cherry
Smoking Time: 30 minutes for the shrimp

Ingredients:
For the Shrimp:
1 pound large shrimp, peeled and deveined
2 tablespoons olive oil
1 teaspoon smoked paprika
1/2 teaspoon garlic powder
1/4 teaspoon cayenne pepper (adjust to taste)
Salt and freshly ground black pepper, to taste
For the Grits:
1 cup stone-ground grits
4 cups water or chicken broth (for more flavor)
1 cup sharp cheddar cheese, grated
1/4 cup Parmesan cheese, grated
2 tablespoons unsalted butter
Salt and freshly ground black pepper, to taste
For the Garnish:
4 slices bacon, cooked and crumbled
1/4 cup green onions, chopped
Additional grated sharp cheddar cheese, for serving

Instructions:
- In a bowl, combine shrimp with olive oil, smoked paprika, garlic powder, cayenne pepper, salt, and black pepper. Toss to coat evenly. Set aside to marinate for about 15 minutes while you prep the smoker.

- Preheat your electric smoker to 225°F using apple or cherry wood chips for a sweet and mild smoke flavor. This will complement the shrimp beautifully.
- While the smoker heats, bring water or chicken broth to a boil in a medium saucepan. Whisk in the grits and reduce the heat to low. Cover and cook, stirring occasionally, until the grits are thick and creamy, about 45-50 minutes. Remove from heat and stir in the cheddar cheese, Parmesan cheese, and butter. Season with salt and pepper to taste. Keep warm.
- Place the marinated shrimp on a smoker tray or in a smoking basket. Smoke for about 30 minutes, or until the shrimp are pink and opaque.
- Spoon the creamy grits into bowls. Top with smoked shrimp, crumbled bacon, chopped green onions, and a sprinkle of extra cheddar cheese.
- Enjoy your deliciously smoky shrimp and grits immediately, savoring the harmonious blend of creamy, cheesy grits with the gently smoked, spiced shrimp.

ALDER-SMOKED CLAMS WITH WHITE WINE SAUCE

Prep Time: 20 minutes
Cook Time: 10 minutes
Servings: 4
Wood Type: Alder
Smoking Time: 30 minutes

Ingredients:
For the Clams:
2 pounds fresh clams, cleaned
1 cup dry white wine
2 tablespoons unsalted butter
1 tablespoon olive oil
4 cloves garlic, minced
1 small shallot, finely chopped
1 teaspoon fresh thyme leaves
Salt and freshly ground black pepper, to taste
1/4 cup fresh parsley, chopped (for garnish)
Lemon wedges, for serving

Instructions:
- Start by preheating your electric smoker to 225°F and add alder wood chips to the designated tray. Ensure there's no water in the water tray to keep the smoke dry for a more intense flavor.
- In a large bowl, soak the clams in cold water for 20 minutes to remove any sand. Drain and rinse thoroughly under cold running water. Discard any clams that are open and do not close when lightly tapped.
- Place the cleaned clams on a perforated grill tray or in a smoker-safe pan. Smoke in the preheated electric smoker using alder wood for about 30 minutes, or until the clams open. Discard any clams that do not open.
- While the clams are smoking, heat a large skillet over medium heat. Add the butter and olive oil. Once the butter has melted, add the garlic and shallot, sautéing until soft and fragrant, about 2 minutes.
- Pour in the white wine and add the thyme. Bring the mixture to a simmer and let it reduce by half, about 5-7 minutes. Season with salt and pepper to taste.
- Once the clams are smoked and opened, transfer them to the skillet with the white wine sauce. Toss gently to coat the clams in the sauce.
- Arrange the clams on a serving platter. Pour any remaining sauce over the clams, garnish with chopped parsley, and serve immediately with lemon wedges on the side.

CHERRYWOOD-SMOKED TUNA STEAKS WITH SESAME GLAZE

Prep Time: 20 minutes
Cook Time: 2 hours
Servings: 4
Wood Type: Cherrywood
Smoking Time: 1.5 hours

Ingredients
4 tuna steaks (about 6 oz each)
2 tablespoons olive oil
Salt and freshly ground black pepper, to taste
1/4 cup soy sauce
2 tablespoons honey
1 tablespoon rice vinegar
1 tablespoon sesame oil
2 cloves garlic, minced
1 teaspoon fresh ginger, grated
1 tablespoon sesame seeds
1/4 teaspoon red pepper flakes (optional)
Green onions, sliced for garnish

Instructions
- Start by prepping your tuna steaks. Rinse them under cold water and pat dry with paper towels. Brush each steak lightly with olive oil and season both sides with salt and pepper to taste. Set aside while you preheat your smoker.
- Preheat your electric smoker to 225°F using cherrywood chips to infuse the tuna with a mild, sweet smoky flavor that complements its natural taste.
- In a small saucepan, combine soy sauce, honey, rice vinegar, sesame oil, minced garlic, and grated ginger. Bring the mixture to a simmer over medium heat, stirring occasionally. Once the honey dissolves and the mixture is well combined, remove from heat. Stir in sesame seeds and red pepper flakes (if using). Set aside some glaze for serving and keep the rest for basting.
- Place the tuna steaks in the smoker. Smoke for about 1.5 hours, or until the internal temperature reaches 145°F for a medium level of doneness. Baste the tuna steaks with the sesame glaze every 30 minutes during the smoking process to build up a flavorful crust.
- Once the tuna is cooked, give it a final brush with the sesame glaze. Let the steaks rest for a few minutes before slicing. Serve garnished with sliced green onions and a drizzle of the reserved sesame glaze.
- These cherrywood-smoked tuna steaks pair beautifully with steamed jasmine rice or a fresh cucumber salad for a complete meal.

SMOKED SARDINES WITH LEMON AND OLIVE OIL

Prep Time: 15 minutes
Cook Time: 45 minutes to 1 hour
Servings: 4
Wood Type: Applewood
Smoking Time: 30-45 minutes

Ingredients:
16 fresh sardines, cleaned and gutted
2 lemons, one sliced and one juiced
4 tablespoons extra virgin olive oil
4 cloves garlic, minced
1 teaspoon sea salt

1/2 teaspoon freshly ground black pepper
2 tablespoons fresh parsley, chopped (for garnish)
Additional lemon wedges, for serving

Instructions:
- Preheat your electric smoker to 225°F using applewood chips for a subtle, fruity smoke that complements the sardines perfectly.
- Rinse the sardines under cold water and pat dry with paper towels. Lay them out and ensure they are fully prepped for the smoker.
- In a small bowl, whisk together the lemon juice (from one lemon), extra virgin olive oil, minced garlic, sea salt, and black pepper.
- Place the sardines in a shallow dish and pour the marinade over them, making sure each sardine is well coated. Let them marinate for about 10 minutes.
- Arrange the sardines on the smoker racks. Ensure they are not touching, to allow smoke to circulate around each fish.
- Place lemon slices under and on top of the sardines to infuse them with additional lemony flavor as they smoke.
- Smoke the sardines at 225°F for 30-45 minutes, or until they are cooked through and have a light golden color. The exact time will depend on the size of your sardines and the desired level of smokiness.
- Once smoked, carefully remove the sardines from the smoker and arrange them on a serving platter.
- Drizzle with a bit more olive oil, sprinkle with fresh parsley, and season with a touch more sea salt and black pepper if desired.
- Serve immediately with additional lemon wedges on the side for an extra burst of citrus.

APPLEWOOD-SMOKED FLOUNDER WITH CAPERS AND DILL

Prep Time: 20 minutes
Cook Time: 1 hour 30 minutes
Servings: 4
Wood Type: Applewood
Smoking Time: 1 hour to 1 hour 15 minutes

Ingredients
4 flounder fillets (about 6 ounces each), cleaned and patted dry
2 tablespoons olive oil
1 tablespoon fresh lemon juice
2 teaspoons capers, rinsed
1 tablespoon fresh dill, finely chopped, plus more for garnish
Salt and freshly ground black pepper, to taste
Lemon wedges, for serving

Instructions
- Preheat your electric smoker to 225°F and add applewood chips to the designated smoker box. While the smoker preheats, let's get the flounder ready for its smoky bath.
- In a small bowl, whisk together olive oil, lemon juice, capers, chopped dill, salt, and pepper. Lay the flounder fillets on a flat surface and brush both sides generously with the mixture, ensuring each fillet is evenly coated with the herby, caper-infused oil.
- Once the smoker is at the right temperature, place the flounder fillets on the smoker rack, leaving some space between each to allow the smoke to circulate freely. Close the smoker lid and let the magic happen for about 1 hour to 1 hour 15 minutes, or until the flounder is opaque and flakes easily with a fork.
- Carefully remove the flounder fillets from the smoker and plate them. Garnish each fillet with a sprinkle of fresh dill and accompany with lemon wedges on the side. The tartness of the lemon is the perfect companion to the smoky, delicate fish.

- Invite your guests to drizzle their flounder with a little lemon juice right before diving in, and watch as this simple yet sophisticated dish becomes the highlight of your meal.

HICKORY-SMOKED SEA BASS WITH MANGO SALSA

Prep Time: 20 minutes
Cook Time: 1 hour
Servings: 4
Wood Type: Hickory
Smoking Time: 45 minutes to 1 hour

Ingredients
For the Sea Bass:
4 sea bass fillets (about 6 ounces each)
2 tablespoons olive oil
Salt, to taste
Black pepper, to taste
1 tablespoon garlic powder
1 teaspoon paprika
Hickory wood chips, for smoking
For the Mango Salsa:
1 ripe mango, peeled, pitted, and diced
1/4 cup red onion, finely chopped
1/4 cup red bell pepper, finely chopped
1/4 cup fresh cilantro, chopped
Juice of 1 lime
Salt, to taste
1 jalapeño, seeded and finely chopped (optional for heat)

Instructions
- Rinse the sea bass fillets under cold water and pat them dry. Drizzle olive oil over the fillets and gently rub to coat. Season both sides of the fillets with salt, black pepper, garlic powder, and paprika.
- Fill the smoker box with hickory wood chips. Preheat your electric smoker to 225°F, ensuring it's up to temperature before adding your fish.
- Once the smoker is preheated, place the sea bass fillets on the smoker's grates. Close the lid and let them smoke for 45 minutes to 1 hour, or until the fish flakes easily with a fork. The internal temperature should reach 145°F when done.
- While the fish is smoking, prepare the mango salsa. In a medium bowl, combine the diced mango, red onion, red bell pepper, cilantro, lime juice, and salt. Add the jalapeño if using. Mix gently until well combined. Refrigerate until ready to serve.
- Once the sea bass is done, carefully remove it from the smoker. Let it rest for a few minutes. Serve each fillet with a generous topping of the mango salsa.
- This hickory-smoked sea bass pairs wonderfully with a side of steamed jasmine rice or quinoa and a fresh garden salad for a complete meal.

CLASSIC SMOKED MAC AND CHEESE

Prep Time: 20 minutes
Cook Time: 2 hours
Servings: 4
Wood Type: Apple or Cherry Wood Chips
Smoking Time: 1.5 to 2 hours

Ingredients:
1 pound elbow macaroni
1/4 cup unsalted butter
1/4 cup all-purpose flour
3 cups whole milk
1 cup heavy cream
4 cups shredded sharp cheddar cheese
1 cup shredded Gruyère cheese
1/2 teaspoon smoked paprika
1/4 teaspoon garlic powder
1/4 teaspoon onion powder
Salt and black pepper to taste
1/2 cup panko breadcrumbs
2 tablespoons unsalted butter, melted (for breadcrumbs)

Instructions:
- Cook the elbow macaroni according to the package instructions until it's just al dente. Overcooking the pasta can lead to mushy mac and cheese after smoking.
- In a pot, melt 1/4 cup butter. Whisk in the flour to create a roux, cooking for about 1 minute until it's golden and bubbly. Gradually add the milk and heavy cream, whisking continuously until the mixture is smooth and starts to thicken. Lower the heat to medium-low, and stir in the shredded cheddar and Gruyère cheeses until they are completely melted and the sauce is smooth. Season with smoked paprika, garlic powder, onion powder, salt, and pepper.
- Add the cooked macaroni to the cheese sauce, stirring until the pasta is evenly coated. Taste and adjust the seasoning if necessary.
- Preheat your electric smoker to 225°F adding apple or cherry wood chips according to the manufacturer's instructions. Transfer the mac and cheese into a smoker-safe dish.
- In a small bowl, mix the panko breadcrumbs with 2 tablespoons of melted butter. Sprinkle this mixture evenly over the top of the mac and cheese.
- Place the dish in the smoker and smoke for 1.5 to 2 hours, or until the top is golden and the edges are bubbling.
- Allow the mac and cheese to rest for about 10 minutes after removing it from the smoker. This rest period helps the cheese sauce thicken up a bit and makes serving easier.
- Serve warm as a comforting side dish or a main course that's sure to impress with its unique smoked flavor.

HICKORY-SMOKED BAKED BEANS WITH BACON

Prep Time: 15 minutes

Cook Time: 2 hours
Servings: 4
Wood Type: Hickory
Smoking Time: 2 hours

Ingredients
1 lb (about 2 cups) navy beans, soaked overnight and drained
4 strips thick-cut bacon, cut into 1/2-inch pieces
1 medium onion, finely chopped
1/2 cup ketchup
1/3 cup molasses
1/4 cup brown sugar
2 tablespoons apple cider vinegar
1 tablespoon Dijon mustard
1 teaspoon smoked paprika
1/2 teaspoon garlic powder
1/4 teaspoon cayenne pepper (adjust to taste)
2 cups water or low-sodium chicken broth
Salt and black pepper to taste

Instructions
- Set your electric smoker to 225°F and add hickory wood chips according to the manufacturer's instructions.
- In a large skillet over medium heat, cook the bacon pieces until they are crispy. Remove the bacon and set aside, leaving the bacon fat in the skillet. Add the chopped onion to the skillet and sauté until translucent and slightly golden, about 5-7 minutes.
- In a large mixing bowl, combine the pre-soaked and drained navy beans, cooked bacon, and sautéed onions. Add ketchup, molasses, brown sugar, apple cider vinegar, Dijon mustard, smoked paprika, garlic powder, and cayenne pepper. Stir until everything is well mixed. Season with salt and pepper to taste.
- Pour in the water or chicken broth and stir the bean mixture. Transfer the mixture to a smoker-safe dish or pan.
- Place the dish in the preheated smoker. Close the lid and smoke the beans for about 2 hours, or until the beans are tender and the sauce has thickened to your liking. If the beans seem too dry during cooking, you can add a little more water or broth to achieve the desired consistency.
- Once the beans are cooked and the flavors melded, give them a final taste and adjust the seasoning with salt and pepper if necessary. Serve hot as a hearty side dish to complement any smoked or grilled meats.

APPLEWOOD-SMOKED CORNBREAD WITH HONEY BUTTER

Prep Time: 15 minutes
Cook Time: 25 minutes
Servings: 4
Wood Type: Applewood
Smoking Time: 20 minutes

Ingredients:
1 cup all-purpose flour
1 cup yellow cornmeal
1/4 cup white sugar
1 tablespoon baking powder
1/2 teaspoon salt
1 cup whole milk
1/4 cup unsalted butter, melted

1 large egg
1/4 cup honey, plus extra for serving
4 tablespoons unsalted butter, at room temperature (for Honey Butter)
2 tablespoons honey (for Honey Butter)
Applewood chips, for smoking

Instructions:
- Preheat your electric smoker: Set your electric smoker to 350°F and add applewood chips to the smoker box.
- In a large mixing bowl, whisk together the all-purpose flour, yellow cornmeal, sugar, baking powder, and salt.
- In a separate bowl, combine the milk, melted butter, egg, and 1/4 cup of honey. Mix well.
- Pour the wet ingredients into the dry ingredients and stir until just combined. Be careful not to overmix.
- Prepare the baking dish: Lightly grease an 8-inch square baking dish or a cast-iron skillet. Pour the batter into the prepared dish, spreading it evenly.
- Place the baking dish in the preheated smoker.
- Smoke for about 20 minutes, or until a toothpick inserted into the center comes out clean. The smoking time may vary depending on your smoker, so keep an eye on it.
- While the cornbread is smoking, prepare the honey butter. In a small bowl, combine 4 tablespoons of room temperature butter with 2 tablespoons of honey. Mix until smooth and creamy.
- Remove the cornbread from the smoker and let it cool slightly before cutting into squares.
- Serve warm with a dollop of honey butter on top and a drizzle of extra honey, if desired.

MESQUITE-SMOKED POTATO SALAD

Prep Time: 20 minutes
Cook Time: 1 hour
Servings: 4
Wood Type: Mesquite
Smoking Time: 45 minutes

Ingredients:
2 pounds small red potatoes, quartered
1 tablespoon olive oil
Salt and pepper, to taste
1/4 cup mayonnaise
1/4 cup sour cream
2 tablespoons Dijon mustard
1 tablespoon apple cider vinegar
1 teaspoon honey
1/2 cup diced celery
1/4 cup finely chopped red onion
2 tablespoons chopped fresh dill
2 tablespoons chopped fresh parsley
3 hard-boiled eggs, chopped
4 slices of bacon, cooked and crumbled (optional for garnish)
Paprika (optional for garnish)

Instructions:
- Preheat your electric smoker to 225°F and add mesquite wood chips according to the manufacturer's instructions for smoking.
- In a large bowl, toss the quartered red potatoes with olive oil, salt, and pepper until evenly coated.
- Spread the potatoes in a single layer on a smoker tray or in a disposable aluminum pan.

- Place the tray or pan in the smoker and smoke the potatoes for about 45 minutes, or until they are tender and have a nice smoky flavor.
- While the potatoes are smoking, in a separate bowl, whisk together the mayonnaise, sour cream, Dijon mustard, apple cider vinegar, honey, salt, and pepper to create the dressing.
- Remove the potatoes from the smoker and let them cool slightly.
- In a large mixing bowl, combine the smoked potatoes, diced celery, chopped red onion, fresh dill, and parsley.
- Add the chopped hard-boiled eggs to the potato mixture, then pour the dressing over the top. Gently toss everything together until the potatoes are well coated with the dressing.
- Refrigerate the potato salad for at least 1 hour before serving, allowing the flavors to meld.
- Before serving, sprinkle the potato salad with crumbled bacon and a dash of paprika for garnish, if using.

CHERRYWOOD-SMOKED COLESLAW

Prep Time: 20 minutes
Cook Time: 1 hour (for smoking the ingredients)
Servings: 4
Wood Type: Cherrywood
Smoking Time: 30 minutes
Ingredients:

1 medium green cabbage, thinly sliced
2 carrots, shredded
1/2 red onion, thinly sliced
1/4 cup mayonnaise
2 tablespoons apple cider vinegar
1 tablespoon Dijon mustard
1 tablespoon honey
Salt and pepper, to taste
2 cups cherrywood chips, soaked in water for at least 30 minutes and drained

Instructions:
- Preheat your electric smoker to 225°F. Place the soaked cherrywood chips in the smoker's wood chip compartment.
- Spread the sliced cabbage, shredded carrots, and sliced red onion on a perforated grilling pan or a tray designed for smoking. Place the tray in the smoker once it has reached the desired temperature. Smoke the vegetables for 30 minutes, stirring halfway through to ensure even exposure to the smoke.
- While the vegetables are smoking, prepare the dressing. In a large mixing bowl, whisk together mayonnaise, apple cider vinegar, Dijon mustard, honey, salt, and pepper until smooth and well combined.
- Once the vegetables are smoked, remove them from the smoker and let them cool slightly. Then, add the smoked vegetables to the bowl with the dressing. Toss well to ensure all the vegetables are evenly coated with the dressing.
- Cover the coleslaw and refrigerate for at least 1 hour to allow the flavors to meld together and the coleslaw to chill thoroughly.
- Serve the cherrywood-smoked coleslaw as a refreshing side dish with your favorite smoked meats or barbecue dishes.

SMOKED GARLIC MASHED POTATOES

Prep Time: 15 minutes
Cook Time: 1 hour 20 minutes
Servings: 4

Wood Type: Apple
Smoking Time: 45 minutes

Ingredients:
2 lbs of Yukon Gold potatoes, peeled and quartered
1 head of garlic
1 tablespoon olive oil
3/4 cup whole milk
4 tablespoons unsalted butter
Salt, to taste
Ground black pepper, to taste
1/4 cup fresh chives, finely chopped (optional for garnish)

Instructions:
- Preheat your electric smoker to 225°F using apple wood chips for a mild, sweet smoke flavor. While the smoker is preheating, slice the top off the head of garlic to expose the tops of the cloves. Drizzle with olive oil, wrap in aluminum foil, and place in the smoker. Smoke for about 45 minutes, or until the garlic is soft and caramelized. Remove from the smoker and let cool.
- While the garlic is smoking, place the quartered potatoes in a large pot and cover with cold water. Bring to a boil over high heat, then reduce to a simmer. Cook until the potatoes are fork-tender, about 15-20 minutes. Drain well.
- Return the drained potatoes to the pot or a large mixing bowl. Squeeze the smoked garlic cloves out of their skins and add to the potatoes. Add the butter and mash the potatoes and garlic together until smooth.
- Gradually stir in the milk until the mashed potatoes reach your desired consistency. Season generously with salt and pepper to taste.
- Transfer the mashed potatoes to a serving dish. If using, sprinkle with chopped chives for a touch of color and freshness. Serve immediately as a delightful side that pairs wonderfully with a variety of smoked meats or vegetables.
- If you desire a deeper smoky flavor, you can transfer the mashed potatoes to a heat-proof dish and return them to the smoker set to 225°F for an additional 15-20 minutes before garnishing and serving.

HICKORY-SMOKED CREAMED CORN

Prep Time: 15 minutes
Cook Time: 1 hour 30 minutes
Servings: 4
Wood Type: Hickory
Smoking Time: 1 hour

Ingredients:
4 cups fresh corn kernels (about 5-6 ears of corn, shucked)
1 cup heavy cream
1/2 cup milk
2 tablespoons sugar
2 tablespoons unsalted butter
1 teaspoon salt
1/2 teaspoon freshly ground black pepper
1/4 teaspoon smoked paprika (optional for added smoky flavor)
1/2 cup grated Parmesan cheese

Instructions:

- If using fresh corn, shuck the ears and remove the silk. Use a sharp knife to carefully cut the kernels off the cob. If preferred, you can also scrape the back of the knife against the cobs to extract the milky juice, which will add more flavor to your creamed corn.
- In a large bowl, combine the corn kernels, heavy cream, milk, sugar, butter, salt, pepper, and smoked paprika (if using).
- Transfer the corn mixture to a cast-iron skillet or any smoker-safe dish.
- Set your electric smoker to 225°F and add hickory wood chips according to the manufacturer's instructions.
- Place the skillet or dish with the corn mixture in the smoker. Close the lid and smoke for 1 hour, letting the hickory aroma infuse the corn.
- After 1 hour of smoking, check the creamed corn. It should be bubbling gently and starting to thicken. Continue cooking in the smoker for an additional 30 minutes, or until the corn is tender and the mixture has thickened to your liking.
- Once done, carefully remove the skillet or dish from the smoker. Give the creamed corn a gentle stir to mix in any browned, cheesy crust into the creamy base. Taste and adjust seasoning with additional salt and pepper if needed.
- For an added touch, sprinkle a little more grated Parmesan and a dash of smoked paprika on top before serving.

APPLEWOOD-SMOKED COLLARD GREENS WITH HAM HOCKS

Prep Time: 20 minutes
Cook Time: 2 hours 30 minutes
Servings: 4
Wood Type: Applewood
Smoking Time: 2 hours

Ingredients
2 large bunches of collard greens, stems removed and leaves chopped
1 pound smoked ham hocks
3 tablespoons olive oil
1 large onion, chopped
3 cloves garlic, minced
1 teaspoon smoked paprika
1/2 teaspoon red pepper flakes (adjust to taste)
4 cups chicken broth
2 tablespoons apple cider vinegar
Salt and pepper, to taste
Optional for serving: hot sauce

Instructions
- Rinse the collard greens thoroughly to remove any dirt or grit. Stack the leaves, roll them tightly, and then chop them into 1-inch thick strips.
- Preheat your electric smoker to 225°F and add applewood chips to the smoker box.
- In a large skillet over medium heat, add the olive oil. Once hot, add the chopped onion and cook until translucent, about 5 minutes. Add the minced garlic, smoked paprika, and red pepper flakes, cooking for an additional 1 minute until fragrant.
- In a large disposable aluminum foil pan, combine the sautéed onion and garlic mixture with the chopped collard greens, smoked ham hocks, and chicken broth. Mix well to ensure the greens are evenly coated with the broth and seasoning.
- Place the aluminum foil pan in the preheated smoker. Close the lid and smoke for 2 hours, checking occasionally to stir and ensure the greens are cooking evenly. If the mixture seems too dry, add a little more broth or water to keep it moist.

- After 2 hours, carefully remove the pan from the smoker. Remove the ham hocks and let them cool slightly. Shred the meat from the bones, discard the fat and bones, and stir the meat back into the greens.
- Add the apple cider vinegar to the collard greens and stir well. Season with salt and pepper to taste. Return the pan to the smoker for an additional 30 minutes to meld the flavors.
- Serve the applewood-smoked collard greens hot, with optional hot sauce on the side for those who enjoy a spicy kick.

MESQUITE-SMOKED JALAPEÑO CHEDDAR CORNBREAD

Prep Time: 15 minutes
Cook Time: 20 minutes
Servings: 4
Wood Type: Mesquite
Smoking Time: 1 hour

Ingredients
1 cup yellow cornmeal
1 cup all-purpose flour
1 tablespoon baking powder
1/2 teaspoon salt
1/4 cup sugar
1 cup buttermilk
1/4 cup unsalted butter, melted
2 large eggs
1 cup cheddar cheese, shredded
2 jalapeño peppers, finely diced (remove seeds for less heat)
1/3 cup frozen corn, thawed

Instructions
- Preheat your electric smoker to 350°F using mesquite wood chips. Aim for a steady smoke and a pre-smoked chamber before introducing the cornbread mixture.
- In a large bowl, whisk together cornmeal, flour, baking powder, salt, and sugar.
- Add buttermilk, melted butter, and eggs to the dry mixture. Stir until just combined; avoid overmixing to keep the cornbread tender.
- Gently fold in the shredded cheddar cheese, diced jalapeños, and thawed corn into the batter. Mix until evenly distributed.
- Pour the batter into a greased 8-inch square baking dish or a cast-iron skillet that's smoker-safe.
- Place the dish in the preheated smoker. Close the lid and smoke for about 1 hour, or until a toothpick inserted into the center comes out clean.
- Let the cornbread sit for a few minutes after smoking. This rest period allows the flavors to meld and the bread to firm up for easier slicing.
- Slice into squares or wedges and serve warm, with butter or as a side to your main dish.

SMOKED SWEET POTATO CASSEROLE WITH PECAN TOPPING

Prep Time: 20 minutes
Cook Time: 2 hours 30 minutes
Servings: 4
Wood Type: Apple
Smoking Time: 2 hours

Ingredients

For the Sweet Potato Mixture:
4 large sweet potatoes, peeled and cut into chunks
1/4 cup unsalted butter, melted
1/3 cup milk
1/4 cup brown sugar
1 teaspoon vanilla extract
1/2 teaspoon ground cinnamon
1/4 teaspoon ground nutmeg
1/2 teaspoon salt
For the Pecan Topping:
1/2 cup all-purpose flour
1/2 cup brown sugar
1/4 cup unsalted butter, cold and cubed
3/4 cup chopped pecans
1/2 teaspoon ground cinnamon

Instructions
- Preheat your smoker to 225°F using apple wood to infuse the sweet potatoes with a light, fruity smoke flavor.
- Place the sweet potato chunks in a large pot of boiling water and cook until tender, about 15-20 minutes. Drain well.
- Return the cooked sweet potatoes to the pot. Add the melted butter, milk, brown sugar, vanilla extract, cinnamon, nutmeg, and salt. Mash until smooth and well combined.
- In a medium bowl, mix together the flour, brown sugar, and cinnamon. Cut in the cold butter with a pastry blender or fork until the mixture resembles coarse crumbs. Stir in the chopped pecans.
- Transfer the mashed sweet potato mixture to a greased smoking-safe casserole dish. Evenly sprinkle the pecan topping over the sweet potato mixture.
- Place the casserole dish in the preheated smoker. Smoke for 2 hours, or until the topping is golden brown and the casserole is heated through.
- Let the casserole stand for about 5 minutes after removing it from the smoker before serving. This allows the flavors to meld together and the topping to set slightly.

CHERRYWOOD-SMOKED BRUSSELS SPROUTS WITH BALSAMIC GLAZE

Prep Time: 15 minutes
Cook Time: 1 hour
Servings: 4
Wood Type: Cherrywood
Smoking Time: 45 minutes to 1 hour

Ingredients:
1 lb Brussels sprouts, trimmed and halved
2 tablespoons olive oil
Salt and pepper, to taste
1/3 cup balsamic vinegar
2 tablespoons honey
1 teaspoon crushed red pepper flakes (optional for a spicy kick)
2 cloves garlic, minced
Cherrywood chips, for smoking

Instructions:
- In a large bowl, toss the Brussels sprouts with olive oil, salt, and pepper until they are evenly coated.
- Preheat your electric smoker to 225°F. While it's heating, soak your cherrywood chips in water for at least 30 minutes to prevent them from burning too quickly.

- In a small saucepan over medium heat, combine balsamic vinegar, honey, crushed red pepper flakes (if using), and minced garlic. Bring the mixture to a simmer and reduce it by half, or until it thickens into a glaze, about 10-15 minutes.
- Once your smoker is preheated, drain the cherrywood chips and add them to the smoker's wood chip compartment. Place the Brussels sprouts in a single layer on the smoker rack. Close the smoker and let them smoke for 45 minutes to 1 hour, or until they are tender and have a nice, smoky flavor.
- About 10 minutes before the smoking is done, brush the Brussels sprouts with the balsamic glaze. Close the smoker and allow them to finish cooking.
- Once done, carefully remove the Brussels sprouts from the smoker. If desired, toss them in a bowl with the remaining balsamic glaze for an extra flavor boost.
- Plate the smoked Brussels sprouts, drizzling any remaining balsamic glaze over the top. Serve immediately as a delicious side dish that pairs wonderfully with a variety of mains.

SMOKED GOUDA GRITS

Prep Time: 15 minutes
Cook Time: 1 hour
Servings: 4
Wood Type: Apple or Cherry
Smoking Time: 45 minutes

Ingredients:
1 cup of stone-ground grits (not instant)
4 cups of water
1 teaspoon of salt
1/2 teaspoon of black pepper
1/2 cup of cream
1 tablespoon of unsalted butter
1 cup of grated Smoked Gouda cheese
1/4 teaspoon of garlic powder (optional for a flavor twist)
Chopped chives for garnish (optional)

Instructions:
- Preheat your electric smoker to 225°F and add apple or cherry wood chips for a sweet, mild smoke that complements the creamy, savory flavor of the grits. If your smoker allows for water, add some to the water pan to help maintain moisture during cooking.
- In a medium, heavy-bottomed saucepan, bring the 4 cups of water to a boil. Gradually whisk in the stone-ground grits and salt. Reduce the heat to low and cover, stirring occasionally to prevent sticking, for about 20-25 minutes or until the grits become thick and creamy.
- Once the grits are cooked, stir in the cream, butter, grated Smoked Gouda cheese, black pepper, and garlic powder (if using). Continue to cook and stir until all ingredients are well incorporated and the cheese has melted completely, about 5 minutes.
- Spoon the cooked grits into a smoker-safe dish. Spread them out evenly. Cover the dish with aluminum foil or a lid designed for smoker use.
- Place the dish in the preheated smoker. Smoke the grits for 45 minutes, allowing the gentle smoke to infuse the dish with a delicate, woodsy aroma.
- Carefully remove the dish from the smoker. Stir the grits to incorporate any smoke flavor that has settled on top. Taste and adjust the seasoning with salt and pepper if necessary.
- Serve the smoked Gouda grits hot, garnished with chopped chives if desired, as a hearty side dish or a comforting main course.

HICKORY-SMOKED GRILLED VEGETABLES

Prep Time: 20 minutes
Cook Time: 45 minutes
Servings: 4
Wood Type: Hickory
Smoking Time: 30-45 minutes

Ingredients
2 medium zucchinis, sliced into 1/2-inch thick rounds
2 red bell peppers, seeded and cut into 1-inch pieces
1 large red onion, cut into wedges
8 oz button mushrooms, halved
2 ears of corn, husked and cut into 1-inch thick wheels
1/4 cup olive oil
2 tablespoons balsamic vinegar
1 teaspoon garlic powder
1 teaspoon dried thyme
Salt and pepper, to taste
Fresh parsley, chopped (for garnish)

Instructions
- Preheat your electric smoker to 225°F with hickory wood chips ready for smoking.
- In a large bowl, combine the sliced zucchinis, bell peppers, red onion wedges, mushrooms, and corn wheels.
- In a small bowl, whisk together olive oil, balsamic vinegar, garlic powder, dried thyme, salt, and pepper. Pour this mixture over the vegetables and toss until they are well coated.
- Spread the vegetables in a single layer on a smoking tray or in a vegetable basket designed for smoking. Ensure there's a little space between the pieces for the smoke to circulate.
- Place the tray or basket in the smoker. Close the lid and smoke the vegetables for 30 to 45 minutes, or until they are tender and have a nice smoky flavor.
- Once smoked to perfection, remove the vegetables from the smoker. Taste and adjust seasoning if necessary. Garnish with fresh parsley before serving.

APPLEWOOD-SMOKED MACARONI SALAD

Prep Time: 20 minutes
Cook Time: 10 minutes
Servings: 4
Wood Type: Applewood
Smoking Time: 1 hour

Ingredients:
2 cups elbow macaroni
1 cup mayonnaise
1/4 cup sour cream
2 tablespoons apple cider vinegar
1 tablespoon Dijon mustard
1 teaspoon sugar
1/2 teaspoon salt
1/4 teaspoon black pepper
1 cup diced celery
1/2 cup diced red bell pepper
1/4 cup finely chopped red onion

2 hard-boiled eggs, chopped
1 tablespoon fresh dill, chopped
Applewood chips for smoking

Instructions:
- In a large pot of boiling salted water, cook the elbow macaroni according to the package instructions until al dente. Drain and rinse under cold water to stop the cooking process. Set aside to cool completely.
- In a large bowl, whisk together the mayonnaise, sour cream, apple cider vinegar, Dijon mustard, sugar, salt, and black pepper until smooth and well combined.
- Add the cooled macaroni, diced celery, red bell pepper, red onion, chopped hard-boiled eggs, and fresh dill to the bowl with the dressing. Toss until everything is evenly coated with the dressing.
- Preheat your electric smoker to 225°F and add applewood chips according to the manufacturer's instructions.
- Transfer the macaroni salad to a shallow dish or pan that is safe for use in the smoker. Spread the salad evenly in the dish. Place the dish in the smoker and smoke for 1 hour to infuse the salad with a gentle applewood flavor.
- After smoking, allow the macaroni salad to cool at room temperature for about 10 minutes, then cover and refrigerate it until chilled, ideally for at least 1 hour.
- Before serving, give the salad a gentle stir to redistribute the dressing and flavors. Taste and adjust seasoning with additional salt and pepper if necessary.
- Serve the applewood-smoked macaroni salad chilled, garnished with a sprinkle of fresh dill or paprika for color.

MESQUITE-SMOKED HONEY GLAZED CARROTS

Prep Time: 15 minutes
Cook Time: 1 hour 30 minutes
Servings: 4
Wood Type: Mesquite
Smoking Time: 1 hour 15 minutes

Ingredients:
1 pound of carrots, peeled and trimmed
2 tablespoons of olive oil
3 tablespoons of honey
1 tablespoon of brown sugar
2 teaspoons of apple cider vinegar
1 teaspoon of salt
1/2 teaspoon of ground black pepper
1/4 teaspoon of garlic powder
1/4 teaspoon of onion powder
A pinch of cayenne pepper (optional for a spicy kick)
Fresh parsley, chopped for garnish (optional)

Instructions:
- Start by preheating your electric smoker to 225°F with mesquite wood chips ready for smoking. While the smoker is heating, slice the carrots lengthwise to ensure they cook evenly.
- In a large bowl, mix the olive oil, honey, brown sugar, apple cider vinegar, salt, black pepper, garlic powder, onion powder, and cayenne pepper if using. Toss the carrots in the mixture until they are well-coated.
- Once your smoker is at the right temperature, place the carrots in a single layer on the smoker rack. Close the lid and let them smoke for about 1 hour and 15 minutes, or until they are tender and have a nice smoky flavor.

- In the last 15 minutes of smoking, brush the carrots with any remaining honey mixture to create a nice glaze.
- Once done, remove the carrots from the smoker and let them rest for a couple of minutes. Optionally, garnish with fresh parsley before serving to add a fresh contrast to the smoky sweetness.

CHAPTER 5: ADVANCED TECHNIQUES AND TRICKS

C hapter 5 ventures into the art of refining your smoking craft with advanced techniques and tricks. It contrasts the delicate flavors achieved through cold smoking with the robust essence of hot smoking, guiding you on when and how to use each method.

COLD SMOKING VS. HOT SMOKING: WHEN TO USE EACH

Ah, the smoky path of discovery doesn't just lead us down a single trail; it's a winding road with branches veering towards the subtle art of cold smoking and the hearty embrace of hot smoking. Each method, with its unique charm and techniques, beckons us to explore the wide array of flavors they bestow upon our beloved ingredients.

Cold smoking is akin to a gentle whisper of smoke, caressing foods like cheese, fish, and cured meats without ever bringing the heat. It's like painting with the lightest brush strokes, adding a smoky hue that enhances without overpowering. Imagine giving a piece of salmon a smoky flavor so delicate, it melts in your mouth, or transforming a simple cheddar into a conversation piece on your cheese board. The key here is patience and precision, keeping temperatures low, below 90°F, ensuring we're infusing flavor without cooking. It's an exercise in restraint and meticulousness, where the rewards are dishes imbued with complexity and elegance.

Here is a list of foods that are suitable for cold smoking:
- Cheese: Elevates with a smoky sophistication.
- Salmon: Gains a delicate, smoky elegance.
- Bacon (pre-cured): Enhanced with a subtle smoke layer.
- Nuts: Acquire a smoky nuance, enriching their natural flavors.
- Olive Oil: Infused with smoke for an aromatic twist.
- Butter: Becomes a smoky complement to any dish.
- Garlic: Offers a smoky depth to culinary creations.
- Scallops: Receive a gentle smoky kiss, perfect for refined appetizers.
- Steak (for flavor before cooking): Adds a smoky note before the final sear.
- Spices: Infuse with smoke to intensify any meal.
- Honey: Gains a smoky sweetness, ideal for glazes and marinades.
- Eggs: Develop a subtle smokiness, transforming breakfast dishes.

On the flip side, hot smoking wraps our foods in a warm embrace, cooking and flavoring simultaneously with a more assertive hand. This is where we see the transformation of tough cuts of meat into tender, fall-off-the-bone delights and vegetables into smoky, rustic sides. Hot smoking invites us to play with a broader palette, where the temperatures between 225°F and 275°F do more than just flavor; they cook, they tenderize, and they transform. It's a method that demands mastery over temperature control and wood selection, where each choice brings its own character to the table.

Here is a list of foods that are suitable for hot smoking:
- Brisket: Melts into a tender, smoky indulgence.
- Pulled Pork: Becomes irresistibly tender with deep smoke flavors.
- Ribs: Embrace a smoky crust over melt-in-your-mouth meat.
- Chicken: Juiciness meets a golden smoky hue.
- Turkey: A smoky twist on a classic, perfect for celebrations.
- Sausages: Burst with juicy smokiness in every bite.
- Vegetables: Charred and smoky, they complement any plate.
- Fish (like trout or mackerel): Transform into smoky delicacies.
- Duck: Offers a rich, smoky flavor unique to hot smoking.
- Lamb: Gains a tender, smoky richness.
- Beef Ribs: Become a smoky, meaty feast.
- Pork Chops: Juicy and infused with the essence of smoke.

Merging the worlds of cold and hot smoking isn't just about choosing one over the other; it's about recognizing the unique qualities each brings to our culinary repertoire. I remember embarking on my first cold smoking adventure, attempting to smoke cheese during a sweltering summer. It was a battle against the elements, armed with ice packs and a vigilant eye on the thermometer. Yet, the result was a smoky gouda that became a legend in my own kitchen lore. Conversely, my inaugural hot smoking endeavor was a day-long dance with a brisket and a smoker, a test of patience that ended in a feast worth every moment of anticipation.

Both methods, with their distinct rhythms and results, encourage us to embrace the full spectrum of smoking techniques. They're not just ways to cook; they're expressions of creativity, invitations to experiment, and opportunities to gather around a table filled with dishes that tell their own smoky tales. Whether you lean towards the subtlety of cold smoking or the robustness of hot smoking, the journey through smoke and flavor is an adventure worth savoring. So, let's blend these worlds together, exploring each method not as distinct paths but as complementary ways to enrich our culinary experiences. After all, the heart of smoking lies in the joy of discovery, one smoky note at a time.

MIXING WOODS FOR CUSTOM FLAVORS

Diving into the world of smoking woods is like being a kid in a candy store, except instead of choosing between gummies and chocolates, you're pondering the nuanced flavors of hickory, cherry, and mesquite. But why settle for just one when you can mix to create custom flavors? This is where the art of blending smoking woods comes into play, turning your average smoking session into a gourmet adventure.

Think of each type of wood as an instrument in an orchestra. Alone, each has its unique tone and beauty, but when carefully combined, they create a symphony of flavors that can elevate your smoked dishes to new heights. Mixing woods allows you to tailor your smoke to complement the specific dish you're preparing, adding layers of flavor that can transform the ordinary into the extraordinary.

BLENDING FOR BALANCE

The key to a successful blend is balance. You want to complement your main wood, not overpower it. A classic blend I love is hickory with a touch of apple. The hickory provides a strong smoky base, while the apple adds a subtle sweetness, creating a perfectly balanced flavor for pork ribs.

EXPERIMENTING WITH RATIOS

The fun part of blending woods is experimenting with different ratios to find what works best for your palate. Start with a 2:1 ratio of your base wood to your accent wood and adjust from there. Remember, it's easier to add more than to take away, so begin with smaller amounts of the stronger-flavored woods.

My first foray into mixing woods was a bit of a happy accident. I ran out of hickory mid-smoke and decided to throw in some cherry wood I had on hand. The result was a revelation—a pork shoulder that was the perfect blend of smoky and sweet. It was a hit at my backyard BBQ, and guests couldn't stop asking about my "secret technique."

Here's a table showcasing some of the most popular wood blends, along with their flavor profiles and what they are best suited for. This guide can help you navigate through the nuances of each blend to find the perfect match for your smoking adventures.

Wood Blend	Flavor Profile	Perfect For
Hickory + Apple	Robust with a hint of sweetness	Pork ribs and brisket
Cherry + Maple	Sweet and slightly smoky	Poultry and pork
Oak + Mesquite	Strong and earthy	Beef and game meats
Apple + Cherry	Sweet and fruity	Poultry and pork loin
Pecan + Oak	Nutty with a versatile base	Beef brisket and pork
Hickory + Cherry	Rich with a touch of sweetness	Ribs and pulled pork
Mesquite + Apple	Intense with a subtle sweetness	Game meats and beef
Oak + Alder	Versatile with a hint of sweetness	Fish and chicken
Maple + Pecan	Mildly sweet and nutty	Vegetables and poultry
Cherry + Hickory	Deeply rich with a fruity note	Steaks and chicken wings

Mixing woods for custom flavors is a journey of discovery, one that invites creativity and experimentation into your smoking practice. Whether you're smoking a brisket, salmon, or a block of cheese, the right blend of woods can turn a simple meal into a memorable feast. So, go ahead, mix it up, and let your taste buds lead the way to new smoky delights.

SPECIAL TECHNIQUES: GLAZING, MOPPING, AND SPRITZING

These methods, far from mere steps in the process, are the alchemists' secrets to infusing our smoky creations with layers of flavor, moisture, and allure. Each technique, with its unique application and effect, offers a new dimension to our smoking repertoire, allowing us to tailor our approach to each piece of meat or vegetable that graces our smoker.

GLAZING

Glazing, in its essence, is the final flourish, the sweet or savory brushstroke that adds a sheen of concentrated flavor and a caramelized crust to our smoked goods. Picture the transformation of a rack of ribs, their journey through the smoker nearly complete, receiving a generous coating of a sticky, sweet glaze. This mixture, often a concoction of barbecue sauce, honey, or maple syrup thinned with a touch of vinegar or juice, is applied in the final moments of cooking. It caramelizes under the heat, wrapping the meat in a glossy, flavorful embrace that is as delightful to the eye as it is to the palate.

Step-by-Step Guide to Glazing

- **Select Your Base**: Begin with a foundation of flavor. This could be your favorite barbecue sauce, honey for sweetness, or maple syrup for a rich, deep flavor.
- **Balance with Acidity**: To cut through the sweetness and add complexity, incorporate an acid. Apple cider vinegar is a popular choice, but you can also experiment with citrus juices like lemon or lime.
- **Enhance with Spices**: Now, infuse your glaze with character. Add a pinch of smoked paprika, a dash of garlic powder, or even a sprinkle of chili flakes for heat.
- **Simmer to Perfection**: Combine your ingredients in a saucepan over low heat. Let the mixture simmer gently, stirring occasionally.
- **Timing is Everything**: Apply your glaze during the last 30 to 60 minutes of smoking. This timing is crucial as it allows the glaze to caramelize without burning, creating a glossy, sticky coating that's packed with flavor.
- **Brush with Care**: Using a basting brush, gently coat the surface of your meat with the glaze. Be generous but mindful; you want to cover the meat completely, but not so much that it pools excessively around the edges.
- **Let It Caramelize**: Close the lid of your smoker and let the magic happen. The heat will work its wonders, transforming the glaze into a caramelized, flavorful crust that's the hallmark of a beautifully glazed piece of smoked meat.
- **Repeat for Depth**: For an extra layer of flavor, consider applying a second coat of glaze about 15 minutes after the first.
- **Rest and Serve**: Once your meat is fully cooked and beautifully glazed, let it rest for a few minutes before serving.

MOPPING

Mopping, on the other hand, is the act of basting the meat throughout the smoking process. Armed with a mop—a literal barbecue mop or a basting brush—we regularly coat the meat in a thin, flavorful liquid. This technique is about maintenance, keeping the surface of the meat moist and introducing new layers of flavor with each application. The mop sauce, usually a blend of vinegar, water, spices, and sometimes a hint of oil, is more than just a moisture agent; it's a flavor enhancer that complements the slow-developing smokiness.

Step-by-Step Guide to Mopping

- **Assemble Your Ingredients**: The foundation of a good mop sauce lies in its simplicity and adaptability. Begin with a base of vinegar or beer to introduce acidity and depth. Apple cider vinegar is a classic choice, offering a balance of tartness and sweetness.
- **Flavor with Spices and Herbs**: Elevate your mop sauce with a blend of spices such as black pepper, paprika, and garlic powder. Fresh herbs like rosemary, thyme, or oregano can add a fresh dimension.
- **Balance with Oil**: A splash of oil can help transfer flavors more effectively and contribute to a juicier end product. Choose a neutral oil that won't overpower the other ingredients in your mop sauce.
- **Simmer to Integrate Flavors**: Combine all ingredients in a saucepan and gently simmer. This process allows the flavors to marry, creating a coherent and potent mop sauce.
- **Choose Your Tool**: Traditional mopping requires a barbecue mop, akin to a miniature mop used specifically for this purpose. However, a basting brush can also serve well, especially for smaller cuts of meat.
- **Timing Your Applications**: Begin mopping your meat after the first hour of cooking and continue at regular intervals—typically every 30 to 60 minutes. This regular application keeps the surface of the meat moist, encouraging the smoke to adhere and flavors to penetrate.

SPRITZING

Then there's spritzing, the lightest touch of the three, which involves periodically misting the meat with a fine spray of liquid. This could be as simple as a mix of apple cider vinegar and water, or as complex as a concoction of fruit juices, alcohol, and spices. The spritz helps to maintain moisture on the surface of the meat, encouraging the formation of a rich, flavorful bark. Unlike mopping, spritzing is a delicate approach, adding moisture without disturbing the rub or the slowly developing crust.

Step-by-Step Guide to Spritzing

- **Selecting Your Liquid**: The beauty of a spritz lies in its simplicity and versatility. A classic base is a mix of apple cider vinegar and water, often in equal parts. This blend offers a balance of moisture and acidity, enhancing the meat's natural flavors without overwhelming them.
- **Infusing Flavors**: While the base might be simple, the potential for flavor complexity is vast. Consider adding a splash of juice, such as apple or pineapple, for a hint of sweetness. Bourbon or other spirits can introduce a layer of depth, while a dash of hot sauce or Worcestershire sauce can add a savory kick.
- **Preparation**: Combine your chosen liquids in a clean spray bottle. This method of preparation is not just about mixing; it's about ensuring the flavors are evenly distributed with each spritz. Give the bottle a good shake before each use to keep the ingredients well combined.
- **Timing is Key**: Begin spritzing after the first hour of cooking, then continue at hourly intervals. This timing allows the meat's surface to start forming a crust, to which the spritz can add moisture and flavor without washing away the developing bark.
- **The Art of Spritzing**: Hold the spray bottle a few inches away from the meat and give it a few light mists. Think of it as refreshing the meat, not soaking it.
- **Balancing Moisture and Flavor**: While the primary role of spritzing is to introduce moisture, the secondary benefit of infused flavors can elevate the dish. Whether it's the tang of vinegar, the sweetness of fruit juice, or the complexity of spirits, each spritz is an opportunity to refine the flavor profile.

In my own smoking adventures, I've found that these techniques are not just steps but rituals, each with its own rhythm and reward. The first time I experimented with a bourbon glaze on a smoked ham, the transformation was magical. The glaze added a layer of flavor that was both deep and bright, elevating the natural sweetness of the pork. Mopping a brisket with a spiced beer mixture kept it wonderfully juicy, each application a promise of tenderness. And the act of spritzing smoked chicken wings with a chili-infused vinegar? It added a zesty dimension that made the wings utterly irresistible.

CHAPTER 6: HOSTING AND PRESENTING YOUR DISHES

As we transition from mastering the subtle nuances of smoking, this chapter opens the doors to the convivial heart of barbecue culture: hosting and presenting your masterfully smoked dishes.

TIPS FOR PLANNING A SMOKE-OUT GATHERING

The smoke-out gathering: a time-honored tradition where the air is filled with the tantalizing aroma of smoked meats, and the spirit of camaraderie is as palpable as the smoky flavors themselves. Whether you're a seasoned pitmaster or a newcomer to the world of smoking, hosting a smoke-out is an excellent opportunity to showcase your skills, share delicious food, and create lasting memories with friends and family. Let's dive into some friendly advice to help you plan and execute a smoke-out gathering that will be talked about long after the coals have cooled.

START WITH A GAME PLAN

First things first, planning is key. Think of your smoke-out like a well-orchestrated symphony, where every element, from the menu to the seating arrangements, plays a crucial part in the overall experience. Consider the size of your gathering and choose your meats accordingly. A large brisket or a couple of pork shoulders can feed a crowd, while ribs and chicken wings are perfect for a more intimate group.

MENU SELECTION: THE HEART OF YOUR GATHERING

When curating your menu, balance is essential. Include a variety of meats to cater to different tastes, and don't forget about sides and vegetarian options. Classic sides like coleslaw, baked beans, and cornbread complement smoked meats beautifully, while grilled vegetables can provide a refreshing contrast to the rich, smoky flavors.

I remember my first smoke-out gathering like it was yesterday. The excitement, the nervous anticipation, and, of course, the mouthwatering aroma that filled my backyard. I had chosen a mix of brisket and ribs, with a side of smoked mac and cheese. The brisket took center stage, and as I sliced through the tender meat, revealing the perfect smoke ring, I knew all the early morning prep was worth it. The smiles and satisfied sighs of my friends and family were the best compliments I could have received.

PRESENTATION AND GARNISHING TECHNIQUES

In the world of smoking and barbecue, we often say that the taste is king—and it is. But let's not forget the queen that is presentation. How we present our smoked creations can elevate a simple meal to a feast for the senses, making the first visual impression as memorable as the first bite. Garnishing and presenting your dishes with a touch of flair doesn't just feed the stomach; it feeds the soul. Let's delve into some simple yet effective presentation and garnishing techniques that will make your smoked dishes stand out at any gathering.

THE CANVAS: CHOOSING YOUR SERVING DISHES

Before we get to the garnishing, let's talk about the foundation of any great presentation: the serving dishes. For smoked meats, nothing beats the rustic charm of a wooden cutting board or a slate serving platter. These materials complement the rich, earthy tones of smoked food, creating a visually appealing backdrop that's as photogenic as it is practical.

CARVING WITH CARE

The moment of slicing into your perfectly smoked brisket or pork shoulder is more than just a step in serving; it's a performance. Invite your guests to gather around as you carve, sharing in the anticipation. Use a sharp knife and take your time, letting each slice fall away gracefully. This not only ensures a beautiful presentation but also allows you to share a bit of the process and passion that went into cooking.

GARNISHING: THE FINAL TOUCH

Garnishing is where you can let your creativity shine. A simple sprig of fresh herbs like rosemary or thyme can add a pop of color and a hint of freshness to your dishes. For something a bit more elaborate, consider quick pickles—thinly sliced cucumbers or onions pickled in vinegar and sugar for just a few hours. They add a bright, tangy contrast to the deep flavors of smoked meat.

I recall a smoke-out where I presented a whole smoked chicken on a bed of wild greens, garnished with pomegranate seeds and orange slices. The vibrant colors against the golden-brown skin of the chicken created a striking contrast that captured everyone's attention before they even took a bite. It was a simple addition that transformed the dish from delicious to unforgettable.

PAIRING SMOKED FOODS WITH DRINKS

Ah, the grand finale of any smoke-out gathering: pairing those delectably smoked dishes with the perfect drinks. This isn't just about washing down the food; it's about elevating the entire meal to a symphony of flavors where each sip complements each bite. The right drink can enhance the smoky flavors of your dish, cut through the richness, or offer a refreshing counterpoint to the deep, complex profiles we've labored over the smoker to achieve. Let's meander through the art of pairing smoked foods with drinks, ensuring your next gathering is as much a feast for the palate as it is a celebration of good company.

Pairing drinks with smoked food is akin to finding the perfect dance partner; it's all about balance and harmony. Rich, fatty meats like brisket or pork shoulder beg for a drink that can stand up to their bold flavors, while lighter fare like smoked chicken or fish calls for something that won't overwhelm the delicate smokiness.

BEER: THE CLASSIC COMPANION

Beer and barbecue have long been fast friends, and for good reason. The carbonation in beer offers a refreshing contrast to the richness of smoked meats, while the variety of styles means there's a beer for every dish. A hoppy IPA can cut through the fat of a juicy brisket, while a light lager might be just the thing for smoked chicken or fish. One of my fondest memories is of a smoke-out where a local craft brewery's amber ale became the unexpected star of the show, its caramel notes echoing the sweet smokiness of the ribs.

WINE: ELEVATING THE EXPERIENCE

Wine with smoked food? Absolutely. The key here is to match the weight and intensity of the food with the wine. A robust Zinfandel or Syrah can hold its own against the most powerfully smoked meats, their ripe fruitiness and spice complementing the richness of the dish. On the lighter side, a crisp Sauvignon Blanc or a chilled Rosé can be a delightful pairing with smoked seafood or poultry, adding a touch of elegance to the rustic charm of barbecue.

SPIRITS AND COCKTAILS: THE BOLD CHOICE

For those looking to truly impress, a well-chosen spirit or cocktail can add an extra dimension to your smoked dishes. Bourbon, with its smoky sweetness, is a natural match for barbecue, either on its own or in a cocktail like an Old Fashioned. For something truly different, consider a smoky mezcal cocktail to echo the flavors of your smoker, or a gin and tonic with a sprig of rosemary for a refreshing herbal note that complements lighter smoked dishes.

NON-ALCOHOLIC OPTIONS: REFRESHING AND VERSATILE

Let's not forget the non-drinkers. A smoky barbecue lemonade, infused with a hint of rosemary or thyme, can offer a refreshing and thematic complement to your dishes. Smoked iced tea, either sweetened or unsweetened, provides a robust, caffeine-powered alternative that stands up well to the bold flavors of smoked meats.

Here is a table with my personal preference when it comes to choosing the right drink for the right food.

Smoked Food	Beer	Wine	Spirits and Cocktails	Non-Alcoholic Options
Juicy Brisket	Hoppy IPA	Bold Malbec	Rye Whiskey	Cola with a slice of lime
Smoked Chicken or Fish	Light Lager	Chardonnay for its versatility	Tequila with a splash of lime	Lemonade with mint
Powerfully Smoked Meats	Porter for richness	Robust Zinfandel or Syrah	Bourbon or Smoky Mezcal Cocktail	Ginger Beer
Smoked Seafood or Poultry	Wheat Beer for lightness	Crisp Sauvignon Blanc or Chilled Rosé	Gin and Tonic with Rosemary	Cucumber Water
General Barbecue	Amber Ale	Medium-bodied Merlot	Spiced Rum	Smoky Barbecue Lemonade or Smoked Iced Tea
Smoked Ribs	Dark Stout	Bold Cabernet Sauvignon	Rum-based Cocktails	Craft Root Beer

Smoked Vegetables	Saison or Farmhouse Ale	Light Pinot Noir	Vodka Martinis	Herbal Iced Teas
Smoked Cheese	Fruity Lambic	Sparkling Wine	Aged Whiskey	Sparkling Water with Citrus

The joy of pairing drinks with smoked foods is in the experimentation, the discovery of combinations that surprise and delight. It's about enhancing the communal experience of sharing a meal, where every sip and every bite contribute to the tapestry of flavors and memories being created. So, the next time you're planning your smoke-out menu, give as much thought to the drinks as you do to the dishes.

CHAPTER 7: TROUBLESHOOTING COMMON ELECTRIC SMOKER PROBLEMS

As we transition from how to host and present your smoked masterpieces, we delve into the practical wisdom of Chapter 7, addressing the inevitable curveballs and troubleshooting queries that come with electric smoking.

COMMON ISSUES AND HOW TO SOLVE THEM

Embarking on the electric smoking journey can sometimes feel like navigating a ship through misty waters—you know there's smooth sailing ahead, but occasionally you might hit a snag. Fear not, fellow smoke enthusiasts! Like any great adventure, the path to smoking mastery comes with its share of challenges, but also with solutions that make us wiser and our meals even more delicious. Let's tackle some common electric smoker problems together, sharing tales and tips to keep our smoking voyage on course.

WHEN THE HEAT JUST ISN'T RIGHT

One of the most common issues you might encounter is your smoker not reaching the desired temperature or, conversely, getting too hot. Before you start troubleshooting, remember the golden rule of electric smokers: patience is a virtue. These machines can take time to adjust, especially in colder weather.

The Fix: Check your smoker's vent positions; improper airflow can lead to temperature inconsistencies. Ensure your heating element is clean and unobstructed, and always preheat your smoker for the best results. A cover can also help maintain temperature in windy or cold conditions. And remember, an external thermometer can be your best friend, giving you a second opinion when your smoker's built-in gauge seems off.

WHEN THE SMOKE JUST WON'T FLOW

Ah, smoke—the heart and soul of our craft. But what to do when your smoker seems more like a steam engine, puffing out clear air instead of that rich, flavorful smoke?

The Fix: First, check your wood chips. Are they dry? Moisture can be a smoke-stopper. If they're looking good, then consider the type and size of wood you're using. Sometimes, finer chips or a different wood variety can make all the difference. And don't forget airflow; too little and your chips won't smolder as they should. Adjust your vents and experiment to find the sweet spot.

WHEN THE ELEMENT WON'T HEAT

Encountering a cold smoker when you're ready to embark on your smoking journey can cool your spirits faster than a brisket freezes in winter.

The Fix: This often boils down to electrical issues. Ensure your smoker is properly connected and that your outlet is delivering power. Sometimes, a smoker's heating element can wear out, requiring a replacement. While this might seem daunting, it's a straightforward fix that can breathe new life into your smoker. And always, safety first—when in doubt, consulting a professional or the manufacturer's guidance is the way to go.

WHEN THE SMOKE FLAVOR OVERWHELMS

Ever taken a bite of your smoked masterpiece only to find it tastes like you're gnawing on a charcoal briquette? Over-smoking can lead to bitter flavors, overshadowing the nuanced taste of your carefully chosen cuts.

The Fix: Moderation is key. Use fewer wood chips and smoke for shorter durations, especially when working with delicate meats like fish or chicken. Remember, you can always add more smoke, but you can't take it away once it's there. It's all about finding that perfect balance that sings to your taste buds.

Every problem encountered on the path to smoking perfection is not just a hurdle; it's an opportunity to learn, adapt, and ultimately, to savor the victories that much more. I still chuckle when I think back to my early days of smoking, when I spent an entire afternoon troubleshooting what I thought was a broken smoker, only to realize I'd tripped the kitchen GFCI outlet. It was a simple fix, but it taught me an invaluable lesson about the importance of checking the basics first.

HOW TO ADAPT RECIPES FOR ELECTRIC SMOKERS

Venturing into the world of electric smoking often means bringing along your cherished recipes, ones that have perhaps been passed down through generations or discovered in the pages of a beloved cookbook. But as we know, not all recipes are created with electric smokers in mind. Fear not, for adapting these culinary blueprints to suit our trusty electric companions is not just possible; it's a pathway to innovation and flavor exploration.

First and foremost, it's essential to grasp that electric smokers, with their steady temperatures and controlled smoke levels, offer a different environment than traditional wood or charcoal smokers. This doesn't mean compromise; rather, it's an opportunity to finesse and fine-tune.

THE HEAT IS ON (BUT IT'S DIFFERENT)

One of the most endearing qualities of electric smokers is their ability to maintain consistent temperatures without the constant vigilance required by traditional methods. When adapting recipes, consider this your advantage. If a recipe calls for a "low and slow" approach, an electric smoker can be your best ally, maintaining the perfect temperature without the need for constant adjustments.

I once took on the challenge of adapting my grandfather's brisket recipe, traditionally cooked over a pit for hours under the watchful eye of the family pitmaster. In my electric smoker, I found I could replicate not just the tenderness but also the depth of flavor, all while enjoying a more leisurely day.

SMOKE FLAVOR: A DELICATE DANCE

Traditional smoking can sometimes introduce a more intense smoke flavor, especially when managed less meticulously. Electric smokers, with their ability to use precisely measured wood chips, offer a cleaner, more controlled smoke infusion. When adapting recipes, start with less wood than you think you might need; you can always add more, but you can't take it away once it's there.

MOISTURE MATTERS

One of the secrets to successful smoking in an electric unit is managing moisture. Some recipes, especially those designed for open-flame smoking, don't account for the enclosed environment of an electric smoker, which can retain moisture differently. Incorporating a water pan is a simple trick that helps maintain humidity, ensuring your meats remain juicy and your flavors vibrant.

ADAPTING COOKING TIMES

Here's where the rubber meets the road, or more aptly, where the meat meets the heat. Electric smokers can cook more evenly than their traditional counterparts, which might affect cooking times. Use an internal meat thermometer to guide you, rather than sticking rigidly to the recipe's time specifications. Remember, the internal temperature of your meat is the truest indicator of doneness.

Adapting recipes for your electric smoker is not just about the technical tweaks; it's about embracing the spirit of the dish while leveraging the benefits of modern technology. It's a dialogue between tradition and innovation, where each recipe becomes a chapter in your smoking journey.

I'll never forget the look on my family's faces when I first served that adapted brisket. There was apprehension, of course, but then surprise and delight as they recognized the familiar flavors, presented with a new twist. It was a testament to the fact that, while our tools may evolve, the joy of sharing good food remains timeless.

FAQ: ANSWERED BY THE EXPERT

Welcome to the cozy corner of electric smoking, where curiosity meets the warmth of shared knowledge. As we gather around the digital fire, let's tackle some of the most frequently asked questions about electric smoking.

Why does my electric smoker not produce enough smoke?
Ah, the eternal quest for that perfect puff of smoke. If your electric smoker seems more like a gentle zephyr than a robust smoke signal, consider the moisture of your wood chips. Too moist, and they'll steam rather than smolder. Ensure your chips are dry for optimal smoke production. Also, check the temperature; some smokers produce more smoke at higher settings. Experiment with settings and chip types to find your sweet spot.

How can I get a better smoke ring in my meats?
The elusive smoke ring, a badge of honor among smoking enthusiasts! This pink halo is a reaction between the meat and the smoke, and while electric smokers can make achieving it a bit trickier, it's not impossible. Try adding a small piece of charcoal to your wood chip tray or using a smoking tube filled with wood pellets for that extra combustion. Remember, it's about the flavor, not just the aesthetics, so focus on the taste and the ring will come.

My electric smoker keeps tripping the power. What's happening?
Electrical gremlins can indeed be frustrating. This often occurs when your smoker is drawing more power than your outlet can handle, or if there are other high-powered appliances on the same circuit. Check the smoker's power requirements and ensure it's connected to an outlet with adequate capacity and try to keep it on its own circuit if possible. Safety first, always.

How often should I add wood chips to my electric smoker?
This is more art than science, as it depends on the intensity of smoke flavor you desire and the specific smoker model. A general rule of thumb is to check and potentially add more chips every 45 minutes to an hour. However, remember that with electric smokers, a little goes a long way. It's all about the slow build-up of flavor, not an overwhelming cloud of smoke.

Is it necessary to preheat my electric smoker?
Just like preheating your oven for baking, preheating your electric smoker is key to achieving consistent, delicious results. It helps stabilize the temperature, ensuring your meat starts cooking at the right heat. Plus, it gives your wood chips a head start on producing that flavorful smoke. Consider this step as laying the foundation for a successful smoke-out.

How do I clean my electric smoker?
Cleaning might not be the most glamorous part of smoking, but it's essential for maintenance and flavor. Wait until the smoker cools down, then remove the racks and water pan, washing them with soapy water. Wipe down the interior with a damp cloth to remove residue. For stubborn spots, a mixture of water and apple cider vinegar can work wonders. Regular cleaning keeps flavors fresh and your smoker ready for its next adventure.

INDEX

Made in the USA
Columbia, SC
16 November 2024

46724875R00061